I HAD NO FATHER BUT GOD

Unless otherwise indicated, all Scripture quotations are from the King
James Version of the Bible. Verses marked (Living Bible) are taken from
The Living Bible ©1971. Used by permission of Tyndale House
Publishers, Inc., Wheaton, IL 60189. All rights reserved. Verses marked
(NASB) are taken from the New American Standard Bible,
©1960,1962,1963,1968, 1971, 1973, 1975, 1977 by The Lockman
Foundation. Used by permission. Verses marked (NKJV) are taken from
the New King James Version of The Holy Bible ©1985 by Thomas
Nelson, Inc. Used by permission.

Cover background: Scala/Art Resource, NY.
Michelangelo, Creation of Adam. Vatican, Sistine Chapel.

Library of Congress Cataloging in Publication Data
93-060289

Printed in the United States of America

ISBN 0-9636407-0-4

10 9 8 7 6 5 4 3 2 1

I Had No Father But God

A PERSONAL LETTER TO MY TWO SONS

FROM

PAUL F. CROUCH, SR.

I lovingly dedicate this book to my two sons:

Paul Franklin Crouch, Jr. and Matthew Wendell Crouch

and to my children's children:

Brandon Paul Crouch
Brittany Brianne Crouch
Carra Linda Crouch
Matthew Caylan Crouch

and to their mother Janice Bethany Crouch
who gave them to me.

*O God you have held me from my
earliest childhood—and I have
constantly testified to others of the
wonderful things you do. And now that
I am old and gray, don't forsake me.
Give me time to tell this
new generation—
and their children too—about all
your mighty miracles.
Psalms 17:17, 18 (Living Bible)*

TO MY TWO SONS

It came from your Father,
It was all he had to give,
So it's yours to use and cherish
As long as you may live.

If you lose the watch he gave you
It can always be replaced,
But a black mark on your name, son,
Can never be erased.

It was clean the day you took it
And a worthy name to bear,
When I got it from my Father
There was no dishonor there.

So make sure you guard it wisely…
After all is said and done,
You'll be glad the name is spotless
When you give it to your son.

(Author Unknown)

TABLE OF CONTENTS

FOREWORD BY
DR. JACK W. HAYFORD

*He who is not against us
is on our side.*
Mark 9:40 (NKJV)

You have just opened a volatile book—one that holds some highly explosive, combustible material. This introduction is a warning. Not a warning to lay it down, but to let its contents work. Let me explain.

Paul Crouch called me: "Pastor, Jan and I felt we would like you to read my new book and raise questions, make suggestions or give me correction. It will be going to the printers in a few days—I know you're busy, but would you. . . ?"

I was unhesitating and immediate. "Absolutely, Paul!"

My schedule had never been more full, time never more precious, but I knew I needed to do it for two reasons. First, because Paul was appealing to me as "his pastor," and second, because he had added that he was writing very forthrightly about a number of people involved and many of the struggles undergone during the 20 years since he founded Trinity Broadcasting Network.

As for the first reason, I felt a holy obligation under Christ to serve his request if I could. Paul and Jan have referred to me as "Pastor" in a personal sense for many years, but it's likely that most people wouldn't know the nature of that relationship. In the pages of the story which follow, Paul tells how it began, so I'll leave that part of it to him. What he doesn't tell is how God dealt with me about them—Paul and Jan—and how that dealing affected my feelings toward the whole Body of Christ.

I had not met them yet on that day nearly 20 years ago. When I walked into the den at our house, no one was in the room, but the television was on, and the Crouches were there on the screen. I'd seen their broadcast a few times—sent from a single small station somewhere down in Orange County, California, about 60 miles away from The Church On The Way, where I have now pastored for nearly a quarter century.

Pardon my frankness (many of you have heard me tell this over TV before), but as I gazed at the screen I was inwardly irritated. It wasn't anything that was said, it was simply that the Crouches didn't suit my taste. Everything seemed so "overdone"—from their style, to the set, to Paul's suit and Jan's makeup. Though I had my opinion, I was Christian enough not to have ever spoken anything against them, but not enough to recognize the subtlety of the Adversary's spirit of judgmentalism which had crept into my soul. As I moved toward the TV set to turn the switch off, a gentle but probing voice whispered within my heart: *"You don't approve of the way I created them, do you?"*

I was stopped in my tracks; stunned by the sudden awareness of the fact that God Almighty Himself had been monitoring my soul, and that He now stepped forward to make a very pointed correction.

To describe my response could sound "overdone" its own way, were I to attempt a complete description of what followed. But I had instantaneously been smitten with such conviction for the smallness of my soul, I could hardly walk. I stumbled from the den to the living room, crumpled to my knees there, and then prostrated myself on the floor—alone before God...and weeping. Without elaborating my prayer, it's enough to say that I recognized the horrible way our humanity is tempted—certainly mine—to "sit in judgment on the Creator's unique workings in different ones of his sons and daughters." I suddenly saw that this was the same spirit which rose within Lucifer when he said, "I will be as God," for he was essentially presuming the right to create beings in *his* image. I wept, perceiving the awfulness of the lie veiled in any human notion that *"people ought to be like I think they should be"*; the blind-minded that idea it was *my* business to disapprove of any who didn't fit *my* preferences—*my* image! And then, with tears, I recanted any claim to *ever* again give place to such sinful arrogance.

Let me hasten to say that God did *not* impress me

with the idea that everything Paul and Jan Crouch did was flawless or perfect in His sight. He simply asserted that they were HIS—by His creative right as their Maker and by His redeeming purchase and call in Christ. He removed them from the circle of my judgment and into the circle of my love. And though we still had never met, I instantly felt a heart-humbling and loving commitment to them as their brother in Jesus our Lord.

Through this experience, I began to discover how impacting this same attitude had been on my feeling toward other leaders in the Body of Christ, as well as people of marked difference from myself, whether renowned or not. As I yielded to the Holy Spirit, my heart began to change—dramatically. I decided to pay the price—and there *is* one—of seeking to always live within Jesus' words, even when some may not understand that decision; the words: "He who is not against us is on our side." My understanding had been quickened by His Spirit, and I now realized I was to steadfastly resist the intrusion of an "adversary spirit" into my attitudes; a spirit which more pervades the mindset of Christians than is generally recognized.

An "adversary spirit," to my understanding, is one that is bound to separate, divide and criticize other Christians, and always for "self-justifying" reasons— that is, reasons which you and I may think right, proper or worthy. It may be over doctrinal differences (not *error*), which *should* be judged, but *emphasis* which may be unique to the individual; or such attitudes may simply run from disapproval or distaste for an individual's personality, style, and mannerisms to their church affiliation or any of the numerous other things that distinguish each of us from the other.

I eventually came to learn that to refuse the "adversary spirit" can bring you under the judgment of others, simply because you refuse to make *their* enemies *yours*! For example, there are many Bible teachers whose emphasis disturbs me but who I will not oppose, simply because they aren't against Jesus! And because I have generally been favored throughout the Body of Christ with a reputation for biblical balance in my preaching and teaching, I will often be urged to stance myself against others of special emphasis or idiosyncratic style. But at the price of the critics' disapproval, I've committed to leave to the Holy Spirit those whose emphasis or style seems "off center" to me. And my tolerance is motivated— indeed, *required*—for this one reason alone: *"He that isn't against us is on our side!"*

The unusual encounter with me which Paul relates in this book, occurred some time later; that moment I happened to be kneeling beside him at a prayer meeting. We were hardly acquainted at all at the time, and how he happened to ask me to be "his pastor" is his story to tell. But it was my decision to make as to whether I would accept his request.

I did so, not because he and Jan would or could attend my congregation (too far away), and not because the elders of our church could be charged with any authority or accountability for their lives or ministry. I simply said, "Yes" because I saw another imperfect servant of Christ like myself, reaching out as though to say, "Sometimes I need somebody to pray with, to correct me, to encourage or assist me in tough decisions—to help me be a better man, a better husband or a better father." I couldn't say "No" to an honest heart, humble enough to admit its finiteness, although the man was obviously gifted, capable, and anointed (and eventually renowned).

So in the limited sense the above describes, I became "Paul's and Jan's Pastor." And on at least a dozen occasions over the past nearly-two-decades, Anna and I have sat with them, helping them deal with tough times, praying with them over hard decisions, or responding to them as shepherds when comfort was needed. I've been confrontive with Paul on a few occasions, too, and I admire any Christian leader who will invite someone to speak with him when he knows that person may challenge what he's doing.

Which is why Paul asked me to read this book.

"Pastor," he said, "because I'm mentioning a number of the hard things that have taken place, naming people and expressing my feelings, I want to ask you to examine what I've written to see if you think I'm being unkind or unchristian in any way."

"Paul," I first responded, "I'll be glad to critique the manuscript. But may I begin by saying first: You need to send any portion of the book where you mention a key person to *that* person for their examination. I'm not saying you need to let them rewrite your book, but you do need to let them know what you're saying and at least allow their feedback."

He only hesitated a moment, then, "You're right— that *is* the right thing to do. I'll set that in motion immediately." And it's *that* willingness to seek to do the right thing that I appreciate in Paul Crouch. I don't know a stronger man than this tough-hided, German temperamented, business-minded Christian leader. But neither do I know of any brother in Christ less ready to insist on his own righteousness or more ready to accept refocusing or correction at crucial points. And I don't know a man more committed or more consumed with reaching his generation with the Gospel of God's love in Jesus Christ.

As I was reading these pages you're about to enter, I winced a few times at what has been related of storm, stress and strain between people. But I was also pleased to discover reconciliation and redemption occurring between parties who earlier had wrestled with human failure, temper, blindedness or self-serving tactics. Not every dispute referenced here has been fully settled, but in every case I believe the writing of this book will assist toward the refining of relationships and the strengthening of the whole Body of Christ.

Paul and Jan Crouch have been raised up by God to do a most unique work in this generation, and it inevitably requires a most unique pair of personalities to accomplish that work. I'm grateful for their obedience to their call and for their persistence in pursuing it. But most of all, I'm grateful for their willingness to keep growing in Jesus—to keep "the heart of a child" so the Holy Spirit may not only speak to them and use them dramatically, but to also allow him to teach and correct them as a son and daughter of our Heavenly Father.

So, let me introduce you to Paul—our brother, and to this book—his testimony. I said at the beginning, "This is a volatile book." So, now, let me interpret *how* it is explosive and combustible in its potential. It can, if you'll let it, *explode* preconceptions and smallness of soul, as God did in me those years ago. It can also *ignite* a flame of new love in your heart for Christ, His Church and His servants as you share the story of one man's growth in grace.

Paul has written it to his two sons, but it's a story *every* son and daughter of the Most High will both enjoy and profit from reading. And I think you'll find it far more than the beautiful testimony it is: you'll find it a teaching instrument drawing you, as it has drawn me, closer to the heart of God—the Father of us all.

One of Christ's shepherds,

Jack W. Hayford, Pastor
The Church On The Way
Van Nuys, California

INTRODUCTION

To my dear sons, Paul Jr. and Matthew, I write this account of the calling of God and the miraculous birth of what has become the TRINITY BROADCASTING NETWORK, with mixed and at times tormented emotions. For several years I have wrestled with the concept of this account as to how it should be presented and even *IF* it should be recorded. In your early teens you were both a vital part of TBN's birth and development—indeed it was your comfort, love, support, and yes, even your humor that kept your mother and me from checking into the psychiatric ward of *"Happy Acres"* at times! But, of course, most of the behind the scenes struggles, battles, conflicts, and at times despair we spared you from because of your tender years.

I can tell you, now that you are both spiritually and physically strong young men with families of your own, the FULL story of how God brought us through the deep waters, the fiery furnaces, the lion's dens, even what seemed to be the pits of Hell itself to establish one of the greatest voices for God in the history of the world. I'm sure some will take issue with this statement, but I speak not only in the spiritual sense but also with the knowledge that this great voice is able to access multiplied millions simultaneously around the world! This is, indeed, the first generation that has even had the technology to accomplish this.

By the way, I could not be more proud of you both—to see God's hand and calling on you—now working in your own ministries and yet still contributing in so many ways to the continued growth and expansion of TBN. A couple of "chips off the old block," say what? I guess dads do like to take a little credit for their son's success, but it seems I hear your mother's sweet voice somewhere in the background too!

So why am I writing this detailed account of the miraculous birth and development of TBN to you? Most of all to encourage you and to tell you of a God that is more than able—abundantly able to bring you through every fiery trial, "MORE THAN A CONQUEROR" through Jesus Christ!

Also, to warn you of some pitfalls, dangers, disappointments and traps of the evil one that await you, too, up the road!

I suppose the hardest lessons your mother and I had to learn in all of our experiences was the tragic fact that most of our hurt, pain, discouragement, and disappointments came from—I think you already know—our brothers and sisters in Christ! Oh the world has hurled many a missile too—you expect it from them—but when it comes from those you love the most, well the pain is indescribable. I have taken much comfort from the story of Joseph and his brothers. When their father, Jacob, favored his one son with a coat of "many colors"—you know the story well! The jealous rage that followed is one of the most tragic and yet one of the most triumphant stories in the Bible.

Well, Christian television has surely been our modern day "coat of many colors"! Why God chose to call your mother and me into this highly specialized ministry is a mystery known only to Him. There have been times when this "coat" has felt more like a curse than a blessing. I have cried out to God on more than one occasion to take it back—to let this cup pass—but then the cloud would lift, the "Red Sea" would open, the morning would dawn. To our wonder and amazement another great station would sign on the air! A satellite was born! Holy Beamers rolled off the assembly line! Foreign nations began to open up—a night when I would throw a thousand salvation slips into the air in ecstasy as partners rejoiced from coast-to-coast! *Ah, the memories—the miracles that only God could have brought to pass.*

Surely "God has chosen the foolish things to confound the wise...." Surely God wanted the world to see that TBN was HIS miracle so that, *"No flesh should glory in his presence." (I Corinthians 1:27, 29)*

You are probably already aware that some very

well-known names of Christian brothers and sisters will fill the pages of this account. Names like Jim and Tammy Bakker, Ralph Wilkerson, Pat Boone, Demos Shakarian, Dwight and Zonelle Thompson, Thomas Zimmerman, and John Wesley Fletcher will have some roles in this drama. Many not so well-known names like Ward Vanguard, Paul and Joyce Toberty, Merv Mattlock, Heath Kaiser, Jerry Rose, Richard Bott, Ray Wilson, plus many others will play out major and minor roles in this drama. Due to the sensitive nature of certain issues related in this book, some individuals' names have been changed. So, I warn you now—some of the scenes will be sad—some will be ugly—some will even be downright funny!

The good news that I can share with you after twenty years of indescribable battle is this: *just as Joseph and his brothers were finally reunited and reconciled as a family in love, your mother and I have come to know the great joy of total and unconditional forgiveness, the blessings of restored fellowship with those who had hurt us most, and the overwhelming success of a ministry that finally gets into line with the plan and purpose of God.*

Finally it is the story of God's great big beautiful family! They really are the greatest, you know. They have loved us, prayed for us, and supported us even when the TV screen was snowy and the set was a Sears shower curtain with two folding chairs! They have laughed and cried with us as we rode this roller coaster together—at the top when our breath was gone, seeing the glorious and dizzying heights of this world. We have screamed with delight and sometimes terror as we plunged down through another valley of testing and despair. Yes, twenty years ago, with one borrowed camera, a shower curtain and only two hours a night on a station we did not even own, our wonderful partners helped us name it *THE TRINITY BROADCASTING NETWORK.* The world laughed—even some in the church laughed, but with 345 stations on the air worldwide—well, they're not laughing quite so hard anymore.

So my sons—fasten your spiritual seatbelts. Our journey begins—the good, the bad and the ugly—but also the glories of a mighty voice that now girdles the globe! *All aboard!*

Sincerely,

Dad

I am recording this so that future generations will also praise the Lord for all that he has done. And a people that shall be created shall praise the Lord. Psalms 102:18 (Living Bible)

CHAPTER 1

I HAD NO FATHER — REALLY!

And I heard a voice from heaven,
saying...write, blessed are they
which die in the Lord...that they
may rest from their labors;
for their works do follow them.
Revelation 14:13

I had just turned seven when Mother awoke me...sitting on the edge of my bed, crying softly she said, "Daddy left us last night...he is," her voice broke trying valiantly to hold back the tears, "he is with Jesus now." The date was June 1, 1941.

Your Grandpa, Andrew Crouch, had been a hell-raiser in his youth. As a rebellious teenager he had been literally "horsewhipped" by his father. You two got off pretty easy after all, didn't you? Hurt and angry he had run away from home vowing to be—*ready for this?*—a professional gambler!

But Grandma—ah, your Great Grandma Crouch— you could never run from her prayers! Grandma was actually the preacher, and Grandpa, the farmer. She packed a big tent on the rumble seat of her Model-T Ford and preached Pentecost from Texas to the Canadian border in the 1890's and on into the early 20th century.

What a lady, your Great Grandma! She had come from a Mennonite background of German stock. I never remember her in anything but her long black dress with the white starched collar and wrist cuffs. She was the matriarch of the Crouch family. Anyone with a problem went to see Agnes Leaming Crouch. She always seemed to have the answer or at least could pray you through to it! Her eyes were transparent blue and it seemed she could peer into the very depths of your soul! You never lied to Grandma—forget it—you felt as if she could read your mind. Those eyes…those eyes! Even a financial problem was no match for Grandma. She could disappear into the bathroom and always turn up a five or a ten. I always wondered— *where on her person did she stash it?*

This is not my biography, but I need to tell you about one Saturday afternoon I will never forget. The rest of the family had gone shopping and Grandma and I were left alone. I was about 18, heading for Bible college in the fall. She said, "Son, God is calling you into the ministry"—you really didn't have a choice, if God hadn't called you, Grandma prayed you into it! "I want to tell you some of the many wonderful miracles the Lord has done for me," she continued. I will never forget that afternoon as story after story poured from this saint of God who, it seemed, was already living most of the time in the glory world. She came back only occasionally to tend to earthly matters! My sons, I will always know that much of the blessings we Crouches enjoy are a result of this saintly woman who, like Abraham, left all to follow God.

The story I remember most vividly was the day Grandpa Frank and their three sons, Andrew, James, and John went to town to buy their first Model-T Ford. Your Grandpa, my Dad, was Andrew. All children and grandchildren had to have Bible names. Your Great Aunt Mary is still living at this writing and is 101 years old!

Grandpa Frank had never driven anything but teams of horses, but in those days the salesman gave you a twenty minute driving course and turned you loose with the infernal machine! Returning home Grandpa lost control crossing the Grand Fork bridge and plunged into the riverbed below.

Grandma's eyes filled with tears as she continued her story. "God spoke to me honey," she said, "He spoke out loud—I was carrying an arm load of firewood into the cookstove when God spoke," again she emphasized, "out loud!" "God said, 'Frank and the boys have gone over the bridge—they are in the riverbed—you must hitch up the team and go get them!'" Her crystal blue eyes glistened as she re-lived the traumatic moment. "I threw the wood into the air and immediately obeyed the voice of the Lord! Sure enough, just as God had spoken, there they were, Frank and the boys—all unconscious, all with broken bones! I loaded them on the wagon," she continued, "and headed home." By now the neighbors had caught sight of the tragedy and had summoned the doctor. But Grandma didn't believe in doctors. She actually refused to let the doctor see them and instead anointed them with oil and prayed the prayer of faith! Her angel face was aglow with joy as she said, "God healed them, honey! He healed them that day—they got up that same evening and did their chores!" For years, the old timers around Woodward, Iowa told and retold the miraculous story of the day God healed Frank Crouch and his boys, Andrew, James and John—broken bones and all!

Years later your Grandpa Andrew in his rebellion tried to run from his mother's prayers but his professional gambler career was cut short in a smoke-filled pool hall playing poker in a little South Dakota town. As he looked up...*across the table sat the Devil himself!* Terrified, he saddled his horse and rode like a man possessed back to the home place in Iowa. There at his mother's knee he surrendered to Jesus and was later called into the ministry.

In 1912 my dad and mother joined Grandma Agnes and Grandpa Frank, Uncle John and Aunt Dora in a missionary expedition to the land of Egypt. God had spoken to Grandma and Grandpa to sell the Iowa farm to finance this first mission's thrust into Egypt in the 20th century.

The stories are both thrilling and tragic. Travel was a nightmare. First of all, it took six weeks by ocean liner just to get from New York to Cairo, Egypt! The trains were antique, open-window railway cars that often passed through choking sandstorms in 100 degree plus temperatures. Auto breakdowns were serious problems with repair parts three months away in the United States!

It is interesting to note here that my father never rode in an airplane, never even saw a television set, and satellites had not been conceived in the mind of man! Surely we are that generation that the prophet Daniel spoke of when he wrote:

> *But thou, O Daniel...seal the book,*
> *even to the time of the end: many*
> *shall run to and fro, and knowledge*
> *shall be increased.*
> *Daniel 12:4*

Cousin Rachel contracted smallpox and died. Her grave in Egypt is a stark reminder of the price paid by those early pioneers. On the other hand, there were glorious victories—churches raised up that remain to this day as trophies of God's grace. Mother told me stories of the power of God falling in those early meetings. One of the great signs and wonders was the glorious baptism of the Holy Spirit upon simple peasant people. She told of how they would often speak in perfect English by the power of the Holy Spirit, praising and magnifying God!

Some years later, in 1936, after we children were born, our own family returned to Egypt, but it was then that Dad's health broke. I was only four at the time, but I remember one hair-raising night! Seniah, our nurse who had come to help with Dad, slept just around the corner from my bed. Suddenly, in the middle of the night, she screamed! Rushing to the bathroom, she grabbed Dad's old-fashioned razor and began slashing her arm! When we finally restrained her, the marks of a deadly scorpion bite were clearly seen. She knew that the wound must be bled to rid her arm of the venom! How strange the memories that are etched in the recesses of our minds.

Needless to say, that night left its mark upon us all, but especially on Dad's weakened heart. The doctor finally advised us that Dad should return home immediately. So I said good-bye to my little Egyptian friends and the only life or home that I could remember.

On the way home I contracted the most deadly form of bacillary dysentery. Our ocean liner was forced to make an unscheduled stop in Genoa, Italy, where I was rushed by ambulance to the hospital. For thirty days I hovered between life and death. A special serum was ordered from Switzerland, but now, World War II was raging. Hitler and Mussolini had joined in an Axis alliance—we were now in enemy territory!

The doctor told Mother that the crisis would

come—the fever would peak and the prognosis was not good. Mother would tell me years later how she saw the shadowy form of the death angel enter my hospital room that night. She recounted how she had literally stretched her body across my bed, pleading the blood of Jesus and refusing to let the death angel come near! The crisis passed and I began to slowly recover. But now, full scale war had broken out—foreigners, especially Americans, were ordered to leave. *We were the enemy!* In my weakened condition they allowed a little German nurse, Heidi Hanover, to accompany our family home to Missouri. How unsearchable the strategy of God. While in America Heidi received Jesus before returning to her native Germany. After the war ended in 1945 she wrote and recounted that all during Hitler's rampage she had conducted underground prayer meetings and church services and had led many to Christ!

Dad tried to resume his pastoral duties in our home town of St. Joseph, Missouri, but a stroke one fateful night was final. My precious pioneer father, your grandfather had "ceased from his labors." For many weeks before his homegoing he would tell every visitor before they left—"IN JUNE I WILL BE WELL!" Indeed he was WELL as he entered his eternal reward in the early morning of June 1. Nellie Pumphrey, classic soprano from Dad's St. Joseph pastorate, sang a most beautiful and touching tribute at his homegoing celebration: *THE SONG OF THE SOWER.*

Over and over, yes deeper and deeper
My heart is pierced through with earth's
Sorrowing cry.

But the tears of the sower and
The song of the reaper,
Will mingle together in joy
By and by.

As we said good-bye to Dad that day the realization seized me at seven years of age that I would never see him again in this life. Now I really had no father...but God.

Chapter 2

Hello World!

Life isn't easy at best, but without a father—well a boy's life is tough. I'm glad you didn't have to bear that cross although I know those years that TBN was coming to birth were hard for you both. I'm sure there were days that you felt you did not have a father either! We'll talk about those days later in this writing and maybe you'll understand better why your mother and I were not always there when you needed us.

Many wonderful souls reached out to Mother, my sister Ruth and me during those difficult days following Dad's death. My older sister, Naomi was grown and married, my older brothers, Philip and John were also grown. Phil and his wife Hazel had remained as missionaries in Egypt and John had just gotten married and moved on into business. The older children helped Mother a lot. I remember Phil and Hazel would send some support even from their meager missionary allotment. John paid our rent for several years—it was twenty dollars a month. Mother was a seamstress and she worked long hours making the blue uniforms that all the girls wore at Central Bible Institute located a block from our little cottage. Every Christmas and Thanksgiving we could count on a delicious turkey, hand delivered by Brother E.S. Williams who was the General Superintendent of the Assemblies of God. What an example of Jesus this man and his wife were. He was later my theology professor when I attended Central Bible Institute. I will never forget his kindness, and his example as a Christian left an indelible mark on me.

This true Body of Christ is really wonderful! They never make the news stories but believe me, they are there—Jesus' true Body is alive and well and has been in every generation.

The years passed quickly and when I was about twelve years of age, one such saint of God was destined to not only make a mark upon my life but would change the direction of it forever. Hazel Bakewell was a piano teacher and also a member of our church, Central Assembly of God in Springfield, Missouri. Hazel, knowing of our financial situation, called Mother one day and offered to give me free piano lessons! I think Mother secretly hoped that I would become a great musical virtuoso, so she urged me to accept Sister Bakewell's generosity. I went but soon learned to hate every lesson. Practice was a bore, the bus ride each week took me away from baseball and let's face it—I just didn't have piano chips in the right hemisphere! But after a few weeks Mother took courage. I would ask to leave early for my lesson and would return sometimes hours late. She hoped that I had finally learned to love the piano but when she checked up on me, Hazel made it clear it was not the piano that had kept me, instead it was her husband Lawrence who had this mess of wires and tubes called a "HAM RIG" in the basement! I spent hundreds of hours with Lawrence calling *"CQ, CQ, this is WØCGJ calling CQ—over."* We would turn off the transmitter and wait. Suddenly through the static would come a reply! *"WØCGJ this is W6XYZ returning your call!"* Amateur radio became my obsession and at fifteen years of age I passed the FCC test and became a licensed "ham." I finally scraped up enough spare parts and after many blown fuses, one which darkened much of north Springfield, WØAVQ came on the air from 505 West Evergreen Street in Springfield, Missouri! The technology was primitive by today's standards. Coils of wire wound on oatmeal boxes, tubes, transformers, resistors and condensers—most everything was hand wired but it worked! I loved the 10 meter band because we could talk to people in Europe, Africa, even Asia and Australia. I loved to watch the meters kick as you talked—also the deep blue glow of the high voltage rectifier tubes—they would flicker bright and dim with the modulation of your voice. I remember so clearly one night as the awesome thought hit me—*"My voice is literally leaping off that antenna wire into thin air and this guy in Japan can hear me!"* I wrote an essay for my high school civics class in which I said I would one day use this invention of short wave radio to send the Gospel around the world. Little did I dream that our weak "ham gear" would one day become Superpower KTBN, a two-and-a-half million watt short wave radio station that today is literally sending the Gospel to virtually every spot on earth from its location in Salt Lake City, Utah. Nor did I dream at this time that those electromagnetic beams would some day carry a full color picture to the homes of America and the world. We will talk about TV in later chapters but I will say here that I was sixteen years old when I saw my first TV set. I will never forget standing with my "ham buddies," nose pressed against the glass of Harry Reed Radio & Supply on Boonville Street in Springfield, Missouri watching a snowy test pattern from a TV station in Kansas City nearly 200 miles away!

Surely God ordains our lives and callings and I will ever know that He ordained this powerful media of radio and TV to proclaim His Gospel in these last days. I will always be grateful to so many who helped me and guided me during these early formative years of what would become TBN! Surely the Bakewells, who put up with me through those early years, will share in the reward for millions of souls brought into the Kingdom through TBN! Hazel forgave me for not learning piano and has lived to see the great miracle of TBN. Lawrence went home to be with Jesus a few years ago but he, too, lived to see in part God's great plan for using those amazing electromagnetic waves to "Give the winds a MIGHTY VOICE—*Jesus Saves, Jesus Saves!*"

After graduating from high school in 1952, I entered Central Bible Institute rather than the FBI academy (which is what I wanted). I knew down deep, however, I was making the right decision. I immediately formed an amateur radio "Ham Club," and with a directional beam antenna on top of the water tower we continued to talk and witness to many other "hams" and short wave listeners. We also contacted other stations of missionaries on foreign fields and relayed messages on occasion to the Foreign Missions department of the Assemblies of God, but just how radio and Bible School would all come together was still not clear.

But then, I chanced upon a magazine article that said: "COVER YOUR CAMPUS WITH CARRIER CURRENT RADIO." *What was this? A new kind of radio station—no license necessary? Send the radio waves through the electrical wires and the FCC doesn't care? Best of all you can tune it in on a plain old radio set and the listener doesn't even know the difference.*

For days we scrounged up tubes, condensers, resistors—fifty whole watts of power! And after a few more blown fuses the thing WORKED! KCBI was born! Word spread through the dormitories—official sign on—TONIGHT! With all the drama, fanfare and ceremony of NBC our national anthem crackled through the wires, and finally those first momentous words: *"HELLO WORLD!"* Not as scientifically momentous as Samuel F.B. Morse's, "What hath God wrought?" or Alexander Graham Bell's, "Come in here, Mr. Watson," but spiritually I see these TWO WORDS today as words of profound PROPHETIC significance. Forty years later God knew we would see 345 TV and radio stations linked together—a super power short wave radio station, satellites, Holy Beamers, and now a great International Production Center to translate the Gospel into the languages of the nations. Indeed—*"WHAT HATH GOD WROUGHT?"!*

But the lesson I want you, my sons, to learn here is that God has a great plan for your lives too. Just as great, just as exciting as radio, TV and satellite. Indeed, if Jesus tarries, technology is moving so fast God may have plans for your lives and futures that could make TBN look like Grandma's old Model-T Ford! I read a while back that scientists are dreaming that some day you won't need a TV set—you'll simply connect electrodes to your head and—PRESTO—YOU ARE THERE! In other words, looking at a TV screen will be passé. The viewer will actually have the sensation of being IN the picture not just looking AT it! But my sons, always remember, these mind-boggling inventions are for one thing—to win lost souls and bring them into the great Kingdom of God!

Yes, there is an exciting destiny for your lives just as there has been for mine. Watch for the little things as well as the big. I am sure it was no accident that I was born in 1934, the same year Congress established the Federal Communications Commission. I've had a love affair with the FCC for over forty years! I hope they feel the same!

God's destiny for your lives is already becoming clear as you both continue to grow in the many skills and technology of television and other medias. You both have already come through some fiery trials of your own, and I rejoice to see the hand of God at work in your lives. I wish I could tell you that it gets easier as you move on toward the *"prize of the high calling of God"*— but it does not. No, it won't be easy, but I am a witness that our God is able to bring you through every fiery furnace, *"more than a conqueror"*! You'll see many examples of this in the next pages of my letter to you.

CHAPTER 3

OUT OF EGYPT

My sons, I told you earlier that this is not a biography of my life, but I do need to tell you a few significant milestones that led to and contributed to the miracle birth of TBN. It is wonderful and amazing to look back on one's life and see clearly why certain things and events happened as they did. At the time some of them seemed devastating—even a complete defeat, but in time it became clear that the Great Master Planner was at work. Here is an important lesson of life: NEVER ACCEPT AN APPARENT DEFEAT AS FINAL. In fact never accept an apparent defeat as a defeat! To those of us who are called of God there is NO SUCH THING AS A DEFEAT! Remember Dad Billheimer? In his book, Destined for the Throne, he taught us by godly example that these so-called defeats are simply "New challenges to our faith." As we grow spiritually, God can trust us with bigger problems!

"God's hurdles," if you please, "on life's track." Who ever heard of an athlete, training for an obstacle race, pleading with his trainer to remove the obstacles? So how can we ever be "overcomers" if there is never anything to overcome? Dad goes on to say, "Let us show all on-lookers that we believe Romans 8:28 and Ephesians 1:11 when 'bad news' is given to us that God is 'big' enough, 'powerful' enough, and 'loving' enough to take care of this 'apparent defeat' in a way that will bring even more glory to His Name when we have overcome!"

I wish I had known this back in 1955 when I graduated from Bible college! Like most of my class I was ready to take on the WORLD! *Satan—watch it! PFC is on the warpath! HELLO WORLD!*

I was just this high when the call came for me to go to Egypt! My brother, Philip, was due for furlough. He and his wife Hazel had stayed on when our family left nearly twenty years earlier. All through World War II and up through the mid-50's they had faithfully served with a missionary legend—Miss Lillian Trasher, also known as the "Nile Mother." Miss Lillian was a lot like Grandmother Crouch. A real pioneer who had gone to Egypt about the turn of the century with no support, no backing of any denomination or missions board—strictly on faith! They don't make many like Lillian Trasher or Agnes Crouch anymore! Miss Lillian had founded an orphanage in the early 1900's which had grown to over 2,000 boys and girls. Your Uncle Phil and Aunt Hazel had worked with Miss

Lillian for nearly 20 years. The stories of God's provision especially during the critical World War II years would fill a book of its own. Some of those stories I was privileged to hear direct from Miss Lillian on her first furlough visit back to the U.S. after over forty years of service to the children of Egypt. This rare visit coincided with my graduation from Bible college. Two brief stories I will never forget left an indelible mark on my memory and have both encouraged and blessed me through the years.

During the war, anarchy and looting were common even in the southern Egyptian city of Assiut. The soldiers of fortune who had pillaged and looted the city now turned their greed toward the orphanage just across the Nile river. To even think of taking from helpless orphans is a testament to the depravity of human nature without God. The lead scout scaled the protective wall to spy out the compound when suddenly from across the Nile a shot pierced the stillness. The thief fell dead—pierced through the heart by a stray bullet! Needless to say his cohorts fled into the darkness—Miss Lillian and 2,000 children were spared by the hand of God.

Miss Trasher told me of numerous times that the children would file into the dining room with not a crust of bread to feed them but with tears in her saintly eyes she said, "Son, we never left the dining room hungry!" A truck would pull up—a wagon load would arrive—always a knock on the door even as little heads were bowed to say grace over empty plates. One such amazing story occurred during the height of the war as General Rommel of the Nazi Third Reich engaged the British and American forces across North Africa. Only a miracle of God kept the German army from taking Cairo which would have given Egypt to Hitler. As the war raged, a German supply ship was captured by the British. The commander knew of Miss Lillian's home and need. A call came over the antique phone one day (a minor miracle in itself) and the General asked if the children could use a boat load of food supplies! Needless to say a convoy of trucks laden with staples that would see them through most of the war rolled up the Nile valley to Miss Lillian and her children. I'm sure Hitler never knew it, but God used even a madman to feed his little ones in need! Don't ever doubt Him, my sons.

I have been young and now I am old,
yet I have never seen the righteous
forsaken nor his seed
begging for bread.
Psalms 37:25

Well, since your Uncle Phil and Aunt Hazel were coming home on furlough, Miss Lillian asked me to return to Egypt with her to help look after 2,000 precious Egyptian orphans. I was elated! Surely this was God—Grandma Crouch, then Mom and Dad, Phil and Hazel, and now me! A missionary to Egypt! I itinerated the summer months of 1955 raising my monthly support. Late in the fall with barrels and trunks packed and waiting in New York the cablegram arrived the very day I was to board the train: *"President Nassar nationalizes the Suez Canal...STOP...Nation in crisis...STOP...All foreign visas cancelled...STOP...Please pray."* My whole world collapsed. Later Miss Lillian wrote to Mother, "Perhaps this was your Abraham-Isaac test. He saw you were willing to send your son to a dark and heathen land. God has some better plan for Paul. Tell him Mother Lillian sends her love."

Remember, my sons, there is no such thing as "defeat" for the child of God. Remember, we never accept even an apparent defeat as final. Little did I realize that this strange turn of events would lead me down an entirely new and different road. One that would give meaning and substance to my fifty watt *"Hello World"* radio station. Nor did I know that this road would lead through an old sawdust floor camp meeting tabernacle where I would meet a stunning southern belle who would one day be your mother! Let's move on—it really gets exciting now!

CHAPTER 4

ON TO SOUTH DAKOTA!

So now what to do? My hopes and vision so high—dashed. I had visited many churches, told all my friends, was on my way—after all Egypt was in Africa and there was a certain mystique, even romance in being a missionary to Africa! I may have even imagined myself another David Livingstone. *Ah youth, what a blessing and what a burden.* Who said, what a shame it is to "waste" youth on young people? I think it was George Bernard Shaw. Anyway, Brother Noel Perkin, head of the Assemblies of God Foreign Missions department took mercy on me and gave me the job of renting the 16mm mission's film library to the churches. It was totally boring. You had to check each print for breaks and torn sprockets, splice it back together, then send it out to another church for a missionary service. One of the films was "Nile Mother," the story of Miss Lillian's orphanage. Every time I saw the title it was depressing.

In the spring of 1956 things got a little more exciting. A series of mission conventions was conducted from New York to California! At least I would get to see some of the world. I was responsible for the big arc light projector and showed the motion picture films in the large auditoriums. It was fun but also gruelling work. Lugging heavy equipment, driving through the night to another city, junk food, little or no sleep and by summer at the end of the tour I was now physically as well as emotionally exhausted. I had had a serious bout with rheumatic fever my first year of Bible school and had lost a whole semester. For thirty days I was ordered to bed by my doctor. Even then he warned me that my heart had been involved and that I would never be able to do heavy manual labor.

One night it struck. I had just retired for the night when without warning my heart began to race. After 150 beats a minute I began to black out. I stumbled into Mother's bedroom and collapsed at the foot of her bed. She summoned Dr. Coffelt who actually came to our cottage in the middle of the night. Try to get your doctor to do that today! By the time he arrived I was returning to normal and after a thorough examination Dr. Coffelt was perplexed—he could find nothing wrong and guessed that I had hyperventilated. He prescribed some sleeping powder and told me to rest for a few days. By now my missionary disappointment followed by a job I knew was not for me had caused me to lapse into a deep melancholy that I could not seem to get on top of. And now a real fear had set in as I wondered when the next heart episode would occur. Again, Brother Noel Perkin took pity on me and gave me a month's sick leave at half pay. By the way, boys, pay—full pay—was fifty dollars a week. Of course this was 1956.

Here is where things get exciting! My oldest sister, Naomi and her husband Bernard Ridings pastored the First Assembly of God church in Rapid City, South Dakota. I had gone to Rapid City most every summer even during high school. Lots of construction work was available in this Air Force base town and you could make $100 a week building houses!

Naomi encouraged Mother and me to come to Rapid City for the month of July because the state annual camp meeting would soon be underway. A well-known camp meeting speaker and Bible teacher, Reverend Edgar Bethany, was scheduled to preach the main evening services. Pastor Bethany was beloved throughout the Assemblies of God, having founded one of the denomination's primary Bible colleges, Southeastern Bible Institute in Lakeland, Florida. Now he was pastoring the leading Assembly of the Southeast in Columbus, Georgia as well as serving as executive presbyter for all of the Southeastern states. Your Grandfather Bethany really deserves a chapter all his own. God had saved him as a tough young gang leader in Mobile, Alabama who had come to break up an old-fashioned tent revival conducted by another turn of the century evangelist, D.P. Holloway. Instead of cutting the ropes and collapsing the tent on the worshippers as he and his gang had meant to do, conviction seized him and he surrendered his life to Jesus that night. His Jewish father literally threw him out of the home so he joined D.P. Holloway's team and was later called into the ministry.

Papa Bethany was the patriarch of your mother's side of the family—the counterpart to Grandma Agnes Crouch on my side. And what a precious man of God he was. His gentle spirit had been shaped by the worst kind of tragedy in his early years and first marriage. Mattie Herring was his first love and had given him the desire of every man's heart—a son. Sadly, the child lived only a few weeks. A second son met a similar fate. In those days the Rh negative blood disorder was unknown—today a simple medical treatment remedies the problem. When a third son was born he lived only a few hours and your Papa Bethany had the tortured task of bearing the sad news to his beloved Mattie for the third time. This time she asked to be alone saying something like, "They need me, Edgar." In minutes, Mattie had joined her three sons in heaven. Your Papa Bethany buried his beloved wife with their third son resting peacefully in his mother's arms.

Papa Bethany cried out to God for over a year that he might die and join his loved ones in heaven. But God had a better plan for his life. For out of that crushing experience came the sweetest, most gentle spirit I have ever seen in a human being.

ON TO SOUTH DAKOTA!

In time he returned to the ministry and met a beautiful little nurse, Laurie Elizabeth Leard. He actually led her to Christ in his revival meeting, married her and this time fathered three beautiful girls —Laurie, Dorothy and Janice. But I'm getting ahead of my story.

I shall never forget that hot summer day in the old wooden tabernacle in Rapid City. The smell of fresh sawdust sweetened the air but nothing compared to the sweetness that walked down the aisle—heads turned (especially the boys) as a slight 98 pound angel seemed more to glide than walk toward the front of the room. Head down—timid it seemed to me—yet the bright red dress contrasted with the retiring even shy demeanor of this stunning young lady! *"She can't be from these parts, or I would have seen her before,"* I thought. *"She can't even be a South Dakota girl,"* my thoughts were racing now! *"Could it be the camp meeting speaker's daughter? No way...she's too...well just too...that dress...but who?"* But as I watched, transfixed, she headed straight for the left front of the tabernacle, up where the district officials and dignitaries sat. I have to confess I did not get too much out of the service that night. I'm afraid I watched the dignitary section more than I did the pulpit. At the conclusion of the service after a very short altar session I moseyed over to politely meet and welcome the esteemed speaker's wife, Sister Edgar Bethany. My real purpose was wonderfully answered as Sister Bethany not only thanked me for my warm welcome to

Rapid City, but—*hallelujah*—also introduced me to—
sure enough—her stunning daughter, *Janice Wendell
Bethany!* After a bit of small talk I learned, to my
delight, that she was coming that fall to my home town
of Springfield, Missouri to attend Evangel College, the
Assemblies of God liberal arts school! *Bingo!* This
was it—my lucky year, but then, the bad news—she
was going very steady with a young man in her home
town of Columbus, Georgia! Oh well, maybe Egypt
would finally open up or worse yet maybe I was
destined to clean and repair 16mm missions films for
the churches. My depression deepened as I said good
night and something like, "Hope to see you in
Springfield sometime." I did not know it till much
later, but I had made a pretty fair impression on prissy
Miss Bethany that night myself. I learned later after
having told her my whole Egypt story that she had
remarked to her mother, "What would you think of my
being a missionary to Egypt?" I'm not sure to this day
what her mother's response was!

Well, summer camp meeting ended and after a
month of rest and spiritual refreshing it was back to
Springfield and—yes—the film department. I dreamed
often of that haunting little red dress that belled out at
the bottom gliding down the sawdust trail but did not
have the courage to even call over to the college to see
if Miss Bethany had actually made it to Springfield.
After all, she was going steady—*rats!* Finally to my
great surprise I bumped head on into my little
"Scarlett" southern belle going out the back door of my

home church, Central Assembly of God—yes, the headquarters church of our denomination. This time she was arm in arm with Bud Zimmerman, son of the General Superintendent of the whole Assemblies of God! Well, that did it! The last glimmer of hope was snuffed out. After an awkward hello and a few mumbled amenities I headed for home all the more tormented by this answer to any boy's dream which now I knew was beyond my class or reach—after all her dad was one of the top officials of the church and I was just the lowly film jockey at the Foreign Missions department and now...*Bud Zimmerman!* Oh there were plenty of other girls. Ruthie Syvelle, the switchboard operator, had a crush on me and I had other dates but *ah—that dress...that red dress!*

Finally it happened. The switchboard gal rang me one afternoon. Ruthie called me quite often for all kinds of silly reasons, but this time I knew something different was up! "You've got a call, Paul" she said rather caustically. "I think it's that Jan Bethany from Georgia." I'll always know she eavesdropped on the call, but my heart was racing too fast to care! "Hi Paul," came the cheery voice. "Is this *the* Jan Bethany?" I asked. "Yes, and I'm calling to see if you might like to attend our 'Campus Classics' night this Friday—I'm, well..." she faltered a little, "I'm singing, and I thought you might like to join in the fun!" Silence reigned for at least thirty seconds. *"Is she asking me for a date?"* I trembled. "Well, uh, sure," I mumbled. "I can change my plans for Friday," I lied.

Well boys, that was the first date of many! I managed another the next night and the next and the next. I don't think we missed a single night for the next thirty days or so. By May, at the end of the school year, we were engaged and had even set the date: August 25, 1957. Don't ever accuse us Germans of being slow!

CHAPTER 5

THE SUMMER OF '57

Ah, the summer of '57—it was, indeed, the longest summer of my life. Each day was an eternity as I waited for our "BIG DAY!" Even my film cleaning and splicing was a joy! The clouds were fluffier, the birds sang more melodiously—everyone was happy for me—all except Ruthie the switchboard operator. I told everyone of the BIG DATE—even my ham radio buddies. Folks from Copenhagen to Hong Kong knew I had found the girl of my dreams—I was getting married! I had long since given up piano but still spent time in Mr. Bakewell's basement talking to "hams" around the world. Hazel, my former piano teacher, groused that she hoped my new wife could at least play the piano—after all anyone going into the ministry should at least have a wife who played and sang!

I made one trip that July to Columbus, Georgia in my little Volkswagen bug just to meet my prospective new in-laws and the rest of Jan's family. I found the legendary "Southern hospitality" to be absolutely true and met some of the most gracious and loving people of my entire life. I cherish many of those dear people to this very day, though many of them have gone home to be with the Lord.

For several days Jan and I planned and dreamed, addressed wedding invitations, attended her dad's great church, North Highland Assembly of God where in another thirty days or so we would be married. I could hardly pull myself away but it was back to Springfield for some final preparations and of course my "films" were waiting for me!

At last the great day arrived! Mother and a few of my friends formed a two car motorcade and we were off to Georgia. My brother-in-law, Bernard Ridings, was to be my best man—*hallelujah*—*we were almost there!*

I really do not have to try to describe the emotions of that day to you, my sons. Both of you have been blessed with beautiful brides just as I was. Paul, your choice of Tawny Dryden, and Matt, your Laurie Orndorff prove that you have the same good taste as "dear old dad"! I think God gave us this "joy unspeakable and full of glory" as a little foretaste of the ultimate wedding of His Bride, the Church, to His Son Jesus. If this earthly experience is only an "earnest of our inheritance" what will THAT DAY be like? Someday, soon, we will know and even those who have not known the joy of an earthly marriage will know the glorious ecstasy of that ultimate union with our Heavenly Bridegroom—*Praise the Lord!*

I must confess that Sunday afternoon of August 25, 1957 is a little hazy and a bit blurred. Jan's precious Papa Bethany honored us with a classic wedding ceremony. The church was packed—the usual tears— why ladies have to cry at weddings us Germans will never understand! The organ pealed the familiar "Here Comes the Bride." I think every time that classical piece is played the next line that some joker made up goes through everyone's mind—"Big, fat and wide." But, boys, I can tell you that line did not fit my bride! Call me prejudiced if you will, but the veiled vision that once again "glided" down that aisle was the most beautiful, the most stunning, the most gorgeous, the most glorious...well, adjectives finally run out. I'm sure my heart was close to hyperventilation once again—this time for pure joy! The usual candles, flower girl, ring bearer, bridesmaids, groomsmen, and vows. Ruthie Syvelle even gave me up and sang the only song I remember, "Whither Thou Goest I Will Go," a sweet and even haunting melody that still rings in the deepest recesses of my memory. The verse goes on to say:

> *Wherever thou lodgest I will lodge*
> *Thy people shall be my people, my love*
> *Whither thou goest I will go.*

The reception was pure agony. I never could stand small talk, punch with ice cream floating on top or tasteless wedding cake, but finally the bouquet was tossed—by the way Ruthie caught it—thank God; then the rice and shoe polish all over my VW bug with "JUST MARRIED" and we were off! Off for a classic honeymoon in the Great Smokey Mountains of Gatlinburg, Tennessee. Do I really need to tell you that I do not remember much about Gatlinburg or the Great Smokies? Just read the Song of Solomon or remember your glorious days of aloneness with your new bride! I can tell you one thing for sure, your mother was a pure bride—a truth you and I will cherish all our lives. Sadly this is a rather rare virtue in these days of so-called sexual liberation.

Finally it was home to Springfield, Missouri and to a little duplex on Hovey Street just a couple of blocks from my beloved film department at the Foreign Missions department and the Gospel Publishing House of the Assemblies of God. The inside joke at the "GPH" was to call it "God's Poor House"—partly true since my salary was $50 a week. Let me hasten to say that I was given a generous raise of $5 a week since I would now be supporting a new wife!

As I told you earlier, I knew that the film library was not my ultimate destiny or calling from God. But during those early days of marriage we were so busy setting up housekeeping in our little two-room duplex and besides we were so in love a shack on the back side of the moon would have been just fine! Even the film job wasn't so bad with a beautiful new bride to come home to!

But, then, one day the call came from Bruce, South Dakota—a small farming community in the eastern part of the state with an Assemblies of God church. They needed a new pastor—would we consider coming for a "try out" service? Jan and I were both flattered and excited! Maybe, just maybe, this was God's plan for our lives. After all, pastoral psychology had been one of my courses in Bible college. My boss was now Phil Hogan, promotions director for the Foreign Missions department. He was probably glad to see me go. You did not need to be an "Einstein" to know that my heart was not in the film rental business.

We arrived in Bruce in the dead of winter. Don't let the "South" of South Dakota give you visions of palm trees! The winters are brutal and unless you are into ice-skating there is not a lot of recreation up there. But it would take more than ice or snow to cool our enthusiasm for what seemed to be an open door— God's next assignment for our new life together.

The Sunday morning service seemed to go well. Believe it or not, your mother and I sang duet in those days! There will surely be an extra reward for precious souls who suffered through our...well I can't even find a word to describe it! I guess you have noticed that we do not sing on TBN—how blessed you are! I even played a little piano. Sister Bakewell's efforts were not totally in vain, but unless it was in the key of "G" I was lost. And lest I forget, your mother did a pretty fair job on the vibraharp, but it turned out to be too large an instrument to fit into our VW bug.

About thirty-five wonderful folks turned out to hear this young pastoral candidate and I gave them all I had!

I compiled a little of the best from every sermon I had ever preached and finally gave the benediction. I don't know what I would have preached the next Sunday since I had exhausted most of my pastoral theology outlines from Bible school days!

The little congregation could not have been kinder. They greeted us warmly and even complimented our singing and my preaching! The head deacon told us, as we were leaving, that the church business meeting would be held the very next Wednesday and that they would be voting on us as pastors. There were twelve actual voting members of the church and they would make the final decision.

Your mother and I, of course, had made this journey a matter of heartfelt and sincere prayer. We really did want the perfect will of God for our lives and ministry that was just beginning. Secretly we had placed a "fleece" before the Lord just as Gideon had done in Judges 6:37-38. We had agreed in prayer that if it was God's perfect will for us to take up pastoral duties in Bruce, South Dakota that the vote that next Wednesday would be a 100% unanimous vote. With that decision settled in our hearts we drove on west to Rapid City, South Dakota where my sister Naomi and her husband Bernard Ridings pastored the First Assembly of God in that bustling western frontier city. Bernard had asked us to consider moving to Rapid City to work with the church there as assistant pastors. The church was thriving. Rapid City was booming ever since the Strategic Air Command base had been established there. Ellsworth Air Force Base had brought hundreds of airmen to Rapid City. Several servicemen and their families were already attending and the opportunities for evangelism were enormous. Jan and I were torn—eastern or western South Dakota! At least we would wait for the deacon's call from Bruce—the business meeting was less than a week away.

Wednesday finally came—and the call. Remember, boys—I told you earlier to watch for the little things, the little signs along the way. Even the great prophet Elijah observed that God was not in the great "wind, earthquake or fire," but rather in the "still, small voice." Often it is the small, almost insignificant things that ultimately determine our destiny.

The deacon said, "Brother Crouch, I have wonderful news—you have been elected pastor of Bruce Assembly of God!" My heart leaped—your mother was snuggling her ear as close to the phone as possible trying to hear the verdict. "Praise the Lord," I responded. "What was the actual vote?" "Oh my brother," the deacon continued, "it was an overwhelming vote, eleven for and only one against—it was a landslide!" Oddly enough my heart was actually relieved. Somehow your mother and I both had not felt at complete peace about this move even though we knew God had some new assignment for us.

For several seconds I sat in silence trying to frame the right words to my sincere deacon brother. Finally I said, "My brother, I appreciate the confidence you and the wonderful members have placed in Jan and me, but

I must tell you that we cannot accept your gracious invitation to be your pastor." For a moment there was a stunned silence—finally the deacon protested, "But Brother Crouch, this is the largest majority vote we have ever had for a pastor. Surely one vote...." His voice trailed off as I told him of the sacred fleece that Jan and I had placed before the Lord. I asked my deacon brother to express our deepest love and appreciation to the saints at Bruce Assembly as we bade each other farewell.

In retrospect I now know that only one of the twelve voting members had the mind of the Lord in the selection of their new pastor. I have often remarked while telling this story, that when I get to heaven I want to look up that dear member and thank him or her for helping us not miss the perfect will of God for our lives. How do I know that? Stay tuned and you will know—by the way, *"stay tuned"* is a clue! But, then, you probably already know that!

CHAPTER 6

GO WEST YOUNG MAN

So west it was for your mother and me and this time we felt peace in our spirits as we accepted the post of assistant pastors at First Assembly of Rapid City, South Dakota. We learned to love the Black Hills, rich in the history of the so-called "Wild West" of frontier America. I already knew it well, having spent several summers there working my way through school. Names like "Wild Bill" Hickok and "Calamity Jane" were legendary. Mt. Rushmore, Deadwood, and the Homestake gold mine are names and places well-known to anyone who remembers his American history. Custer's last stand was further east, but the Badlands and Wall Drugstore are the gateway to this fabled land of fast-flowing trout streams and sweet-smelling ponderosa pines.

While the church welcomed us warmly the budget could not provide a full living salary so I had to seek extra employment for living expenses. As God would have it, the first available job turned out to be—*you guessed it*—radio announcer at 250 watt KRSD-AM 1340 on the dial. I had chatted for hours on end on short wave "ham" radio but never dreamed of doing a real "disc jockey" radio show on a duly FCC licensed commercial radio station! Eli Daniels, an ex-U.S.Navy veteran was the owner and you've heard the expression, "He could cuss like a sailor"? Well, I think Eli invented the phrase! I must say, however, that Eli respected my faith and the fact that I was a pastor caused him to often bite his tongue in my presence. You could always tell, however, when Eli had passed through—noses were buried in feverish work and the air was definitely blue!

The program director gave me a half-hour orientation session on how to be an announcer and disc jockey. "Just play the record and tell the folks the name of the tune and who sang it!" With that he walked out of the sound proof door and guess what? In thirty minutes I had graduated from "amateur" to commercial radio! I will be eternally grateful that no recordings were made of those first days of my new career, but before long names like Jim Reeves, Hank Locklin, the Everly Brothers, Johnnie Cash, Hank Snow and Earnest Tubb became very familiar to me. Country music was much different back then. Most of it was about life, love and broken dreams. "I Can't Stop Loving You," "All I Have To Do Is Dream," "Send Me the Pillow That You Dream On," and yes, there was Elvis with "Blue Suede Shoes" and "You Ain't Nothin' But A Hound Dog." These and countless others became my "tentmaking" as Jan and I directed the choir, printed the church bulletins, directed the song service, taught Sunday School and even did a bit of mid-week preaching.

But then an exciting new phase at KRSD radio exploded! Eli received an FCC permit to build KRSD-TV Channel 7, NBC for Rapid City! Wow—you could cut the excitement with a knife! All of us pitched in—we pulled wires, hung lights, wired TV gear in racks, hooked up cameras and would you believe—*16mm projectors! Shades of Springfield and the Foreign Missions film department.* At least I knew how to thread a film projector which, as simple as this sounds, turned out to be a valuable and necessary skill! Looking back I see so very clearly the hand of God as He put me through basic training, yes, boot camp, if you please, for the day HIS network would be born. We'll move on into that in future chapters, but God saw to it that I would be involved in virtually every phase of building a new TV station from the ground up. By today's standards everything was extremely primitive. Black and white, no video tape, everything was either live or on 16mm film. Even the NBC network shows were crude kinescope recordings which were made by filming a TV screen with a 16mm camera and sending prints to all the affiliated network stations. I pulled the night shift and my favorite was "Wagon Train" with Ward Bond and Robert Horton. If you were into soap operas it was "Young Dr. Malone" and for live programs I directed "Romper Room" and the Saturday "Dance Party." Some of the deacons at First Assembly got a little heartburn on that one so I had to keep my name off the credits!

I will never forget our first TV newscast on KRSD-TV, NBC affiliate for Rapid City. Eli had been after Norm, the radio newsman, for weeks to get the TV news program going. Our competition, Channel 3 CBS, had their newscast with weather and sports and were clobbering us in the ratings. Norm confided in me that he was terrified at the thought of appearing on camera on live TV! He had been a radio newscaster all his life and quite frankly was not all that photogenic! Finally Eli had had it! The call came loud and clear— we could all hear every word from the telephone earpiece as Norm held it four feet from his ear! *"Get that 'blankety blank' news program on the 'blankety blank' air 'blankety blank' TONIGHT or you're all fired!"—slam!* Once again, Norm pleaded, "Paul you do it, you are a preacher, you have done public speaking, I'm on my knees!" All we had was a plain old folding card table and a blue tablecloth. We ripped the latest round-up from the UPI teletype service and yours truly had the distinct honor of reading the *very first* newscast for NBC Rapid City! Once again, I thank God there was no way to record that program—it was awful—strictly "amateur night in Dixie," even though we were far north of the Mason-Dixon line.

Eli's wrath was appeased and gradually we, too,

added weather and sports. The weathercast was the hardest because you had to stand behind a plate glass map of the U.S and write all your figures backwards to make them read right for the camera.

And then there were the commercials—am I boring you boys? You've got to hear this one. Many a night I was the only one on duty operating master control. The last program was usually the "Late Show." When the cue marks flashed on the films I would stop the movie—turn on the studio lights, run like crazy onto the set with a locked down camera, do the cottage cheese commercial, then dash back to the control booth and restart the movie! And you guys complain today if we do not have at least four to six cameras and a crew of at least eight or ten! Give me a break! I guess we do produce a little better quality these days so relax—your jobs are secure! Sometimes I had the luxury of Jan writing out my commercial script on newswire paper and slowly pulling it over her arm as I read the Niagara Cyclo Massage commercial.

One highlight I must tell you about was the time Dr. Oral Roberts came to Rapid City to hold a great crusade for the Sioux Indians. Brother Roberts is part American Indian and for years has held an annual crusade conducted primarily to win native Americans to Christ. This was really "big time" stuff for little old Rapid City. The town, the churches, and the media were buzzing. Oral Roberts was simply the most prominent healing evangelist of that day—this was about 1958. I asked Eli if I could invite Dr. Roberts to

I Had No Father But God

be a guest on my "LIVE" newscast and he readily
agreed. I guess we could say that the very first
Christian TV interview program was aired that night as
we turned the TV news into a virtual "Praise the Lord"
program. Needless to say, the Indian crusade in the
Civic Auditorium was a "turn away" crowd and Dr.
Roberts kicked our ratings off the scale that night. Eli
groused that we had used up too much time for
religious news but the good news was out and there
was no recalling it! Little did I realize that Dr. Roberts'
path and mine would cross again twenty-five years
later and that we would have REAL "Praise the Lord"
programs—many of them!

Well, my sons, I could write this whole book about our
Rapid City experiences but I will conclude with the most
important—the most exciting—the most blessed event of all!

Much to our dismay, your mother began to wake up
each morning very sick, nauseated and vomiting. At
first I was very worried, but the ladies at church just
smiled and said, "You're going to be a daddy!" Ah, the
wonder and excitement for a young couple as they
watch and experience the miracle of new life. I will
never forget your mother's look of panic as those first
labor pains started nor the breakneck race to Bennett
Memorial Hospital. In those days fathers were not
allowed in the delivery room—a senseless rule that has
mostly been changed today. Your mother was a brave
little trooper as she passed through the "valley of the
shadow of death" to give you—Paul F. Crouch, Jr.—
your life on March 13, 1959. I will never forget that

first glimpse of you as the nurse swabbed your tiny nose and ears with cotton Q-tips. You were squalling your head off but I felt ten feet tall as I hugged your mother and thanked her for giving me the desire of every father's heart—a son! We packed you proudly into that same little VW bug that had carried your mom and me on our first date two years earlier and drove you to our little trailer home parked in the middle of a pine tree forest in the Black Hills of South Dakota. Just "Mommy and me and baby makes three"—we were happy in our new heaven!

The next day on my D.J. radio show I found a song that said it best, *"It's a boy, it's a joy, it's the first but not the last...."* I played that record a dozen or more times giving your name and vital statistics. You were probably the best known live birth in the history of Rapid City. Eli finally walked into the control room and told me to cut it out!

Ah, the joy and the memories that flood my soul as I recall the Black Hills of South Dakota. In the natural I wish we could have stayed there forever. We could have grown up together like Daniel Boone and Davy Crockett. I would have taken you deer hunting and trout fishing—we would have hiked up Harney Peak and camped out at the base of Mt. Rushmore. But this was the beginning of something much bigger than your mother and I could have ever imagined—this was *Television 101*—this was the training ground for what would become a voice like no other—God's voice to a lost and dying world. Yes, *"Hello World"* was coming

fast, but that is yet another chapter.

CHAPTER 7

CALIFORNIA HERE WE COME!

The road to California detoured briefly through—of all places—Muskegon, Michigan. Your Uncle Bernard and Aunt Naomi Ridings had accepted the pastorate of Central Assembly of God in Muskegon and had asked your mother and me along with you our new bundle of joy, Paul Jr., to go with them and continue as assistant pastors. For about two years I really learned the ministry of pastoring since we were now in full time ministry. Weddings, funerals, baptisms, choir directing, Sunday school classes, and yes, another ham radio class! It was in my blood—there was no evading it. I even wrote the FCC for application papers for a small radio station but the deacons couldn't catch the vision or the budget! In retrospect, those two years seemed to be mostly marking time, but we did learn to love some of the most precious saints of God we had ever met. It was in Muskegon that we first met a young Jim and Tammy Bakker who were attending Bible school though we only saw them a few times on home visits during breaks and holidays. Jim's mom and dad, Fern and Raleigh were pillars in the church, Raleigh being the head usher. Jim's Grandma Irwin was one of the most Christ-like ladies I had ever met. Again, only God knew that Jim Bakker and I would meet again twelve years later in California.

The whole reason for our moving to Muskegon just may have been for the brief encounter with Jim Bakker, for he and Tammy did, indeed, make their mark upon our lives and ministry that remains to this very day. How strange and, indeed, sovereign are the crossroads of our lives, but that chapter is coming up!

The really BIG event for Muskegon was—morning sickness number TWO! Our little family was growing! By now you were two years old, Paul Jr., and you got excited along with your mom and me as the big day drew near. I wanted another boy—don't ask me why—I just did. Maybe it was the lines of one of the old D.J. songs by Andy Williams which went, *"When you're the father of boys you worry, but when you're the father of girls, you pray!"* In any case, I got my wish and on October 26, 1961 you, my number two son, Matthew Wendell Crouch, discovered America in Hackley Hospital, Muskegon, Michigan. But Matt, you were not destined to even remember the place of your birth due to an urgent call one day from Willard Cantelon, a dear minister friend.

The scene was actually a very sad one. Jan and I

were conducting the funeral of a young father that had been killed by a tragic accident. The church secretary called me from the platform for what I thought must be another emergency of some kind. But the news was electrifying—Willard's voice was excited—"Paul, the Assemblies of God is establishing a TV and Film Production Center out here in Burbank, California...." My heart did flip-flops as I anticipated the next sentence. "General Superintendent, Thomas Zimmerman has asked me to call you to see if you would be willing to move out here and manage it!" Words could not express the joy that leaped in my spirit! This was it—this was what those ham radio days were for—KCBI and "Hello World"—my crazy pioneering days at NBC Rapid City—*hallelujah*—my spirit soared! I knew that Willard Cantelon had been pioneering a new TV series for the Assemblies of God. "Men With A Mission" documented miraculous stories from the foreign mission fields. Though pretty crude, technically, by today's standards, since everything was still shot on 16mm motion picture film, at least it was now in color. Willard was purchasing time on secular TV stations to recruit personnel and resources for preaching Christ around the world! "Willard—tell Brother Zimmerman—YES, but I have to go, Jan and I have just been called to sing at a funeral which is being conducted in the church right now! I'll call you back in a couple of hours!"

Your mother only heard one side of the conversation but had the general idea of our upcoming move as we stepped back on the platform to sing. I felt pure giddy as we began to sing, *"UNTIL THEN MY HEART WILL GO ON SINGING"*—then I began to feel pure guilt for being so happy as we tried to continue comforting the bereaved. *"UNTIL THEN WITH JOY I'LL CARRY ON...."* The song had absolutely opposite meanings for your mother and me and the mourners. *"UNTIL THE DAY MY EYES BEHOLD THAT CITY...."* The mourners were thinking of heaven, I was wondering what Burbank would be like! *"UNTIL THE DAY GOD CALLS ME HOME."*

The song and funeral could not end soon enough for me. Somehow deep in my spirit I knew this was God's next phase for a destiny that was now becoming clearer—GLORY! *California, here we come!*

We said good-bye to some of the dearest people on earth at Central Assembly of God, Muskegon, Michigan and headed for California. Paul, you were two and a half; Matt, you were one month old. Uncle Bernie and Aunt Nonie, as you called them, helped us load all our earthly possessions into a small U-Haul trailer as we said a tearful good-bye on Thanksgiving Day 1961. We felt a little like the "Beverly Hillbillies" as we rolled west toward the Golden State!

Again, I could write a whole book just about Burbank and this wonderful phase God had moved us into. For nearly five years your mother and I helped pioneer a department of the Assemblies of God that continues to this day. We produced records, tapes, film strips, and motion pictures for the Assemblies of God and several other denominations. Productions included church growth documentaries like "Cincinnati Breakthrough" as well as "Light For the Lost" motion pictures that we filmed in many foreign nations. Your mother did secretarial duties and, of course, make-up as we filmed many productions in our studio at 3805 W. Magnolia in "Beautiful Downtown Burbank." We even did some work for the U.S. Army and their series called the "Big Picture." It was exciting work since we also got to meet a number of Hollywood stars and even joined the Hollywood Christian group. We found to our amazement that there were many well-known Hollywood personalities that knew and loved the Lord Jesus. Stars like Jane Russell, Pat Boone, Ty Hardin, Roy Rogers, Dale Evans, Art Linkletter and many others met regularly for prayer and Bible study. "Dear Lord," I thought, "the folks back home will never believe that there are REAL Christians in the entertainment business out here in Hollywood!" Your mother and I were delighted and flattered to be asked to join this esteemed group.

I suppose our biggest assignment was to produce the 50th Anniversary motion picture which traced the origins of the Assemblies of God from its first founding and General Council in Hot Springs, Arkansas in 1914. By 1964 it had become the largest Pentecostal denomination in the world as well as the fastest growing. You boys will be proud to know that my dad, your Grandpa Andrew Crouch, was one of the

founders of the Assemblies of God and is pictured in
that first historic photograph with men like J.R. Flower,
E.N. Bell, J.W. Welch, and many other well-known
ministers in the Assembly of God circles. "Like A
River" was the title of this historic production and it is
still an often used teaching film for Assemblies
colleges and churches. Of course, "A Child Is
Wanting" was my favorite production since it
documented the tragic stories of the children at the Hot
Springs, Arkansas orphanage. Believe it or not, your
old dad *(I was young then)* actually played a bit part in
the courtroom scene filmed in a real Burbank
courtroom with Byron Morrow and Vic Perrin, who
was well-known at the time for his role in the Jack
Webb "Dragnet" TV series.

Yes, Burbank was, indeed, the vital next phase of
this most unusual college of "hard knocks" that God
was putting your mother and me through.

But all good things must come to an end and that
day came when the officials at Springfield decided to
move the TV and Film Production Center from
Burbank back to Springfield, Missouri, the
denomination's headquarters. After thought and much
prayer your mother and I both agreed that we were to
remain in California. It was one of the most difficult
decisions of our lives. After all, Springfield was my
home town, all my friends were there, my own
precious mother was there—my heart was pulled
toward home, but my spirit said stay!

I do not need to tell you boys much about our next

phase of schooling in Corona, California since it was there your most memorable childhood and school days were experienced. As we were saying good-bye to Burbank, Dr. William J. Roberts called me to ask if I would consider managing his radio station in Corona, a suburb of the sprawling southern California metroplex. Dr. Roberts was a well-known radio pioneer and pastor, having been one of the founders of FEBC, the Far East Broadcasting Company, sending short wave Christian radio into Asia for many years. Your mother and I accepted and for the next five years I learned FCC law, business management skills, rough and tough competition with dozens of stations vying for the scarce advertising dollars in the market. This was graduate school time—it was make it or go broke time. There were no safety nets—you got out there and hustled your program and advertising time for as little as a *"dollar a holler"* as the old joke went. KREL, Corona, California was owned by a small group of Christian partners. We did broadcast some Christian programs but by and large it was a pure commercial venture. After two years the partners were pleased enough with my performance that a ten percent block of corporate stock was given to me as a bonus! Wonder of wonders—I was now a radio station owner! Your mother became "Mrs. Civic Corona." From president of the PTA to chairman of the Mayor's Ball, she worked hard to help make KREL the community leader—FCC public service at its best! Paul, do you remember dressing up at about age eight in that classic page boy outfit and reading the official invitation to the City Council to attend the Mayor's Ball? You were a doll and made the front page of the *Corona Courier!* Matt, do you remember coming home from school starving because your teacher refused to give you your lunch that was delivered late because you forgot it? *Boy, howdy,* heads rolled as the PTA hit the beaches! You should also remember that the whole school lunch program changed as a group of angry mothers descended on the superintendent of schools to demand better food and that you kids be allowed to eat inside rather than sweltering or freezing on outside benches because the teachers did not want the mess inside. God was surely toughening up your mom as well for the REAL battles up the road. Yes, Garretson Avenue School may never be the same since president Jan and her compatriots launched their "D-Day" on elementary education in Corona, California.

Yes, we had many happy, learning, growing up days in Corona, but still there was that deep inner gnawing in my spirit that even Corona was only more preparation for that greater calling—that as yet unknown destiny that somehow lay just ahead.

CHAPTER 8

THE MIRACLE BEGINS!

The miracle birth of TBN really began in 1971 with a call from Ray Schoch, pastor of Faith Center Church in Glendale, California. He had launched an FM radio station and had just been successful in acquiring an FCC permit for a UHF TV station licensed to San Bernardino, California. A whole TV station devoted 100% to Christian programming was a radical new concept, but Pastor Ray was a great man of faith and finally fought it through and got KHOF-TV Channel 30 on the air! The problem was that San Bernardino was about sixty miles east of Glendale, which was virtually out of our range. We could not even pick up the signal at the church in Glendale. It did, however, cover much of the greater southern California area. Both the radio and new TV station were struggling financially. FM was relatively new for radio, and UHF—well, in those days very few TV home receivers were even wired to receive it. You had to get that little black box that sat on top of the set—remember? We estimated that only about twenty percent of the homes in southern California could even receive UHF Channel 30.

Pastor Schoch's call came at a God ordained time. I had just sold my interest in the Corona radio station and your mother and I were simply waiting on the Lord in our new home we had just purchased for $38,500 in Orange County, California. By the way, we still live there. It's a lot lonelier since you boys left us, but it still holds many wonderful memories for all of us. As Edgar Guest wrote, "It takes a heap of living in a house to make a home." Well, after twenty-two years of laughter and tears, that little house in Newport Beach is home to your mother and me! I will ever know that God led us to that home since it was only about ten minutes from 111 West Dyer Road in Santa Ana—but, again, I'm getting ahead of my story.

Now, I must hurry because we are coming to that rendezvous with destiny—the culmination of those many years of testing and training—the purpose, I believe, for which I was born. My sons, there is nothing more important in all of life than to find your purpose—God's purpose for you! How many live sad, depressed and unfulfilled lives simply because they did not find God's perfect plan for their lives. That line sounds almost like a super-spiritual cliche´, but God really does have an exciting, happy, gloriously fulfilled life for everyone. But, how does one find it? Well, that subject deserves a book all its own and many, of course, have been written about it, but let me give you two important clues before moving on. First of all, God says in Jeremiah 29:13:

> *And ye shall seek me, and find me,*
> *when ye shall search for me*
> *with all your heart.*

Secondly, make your important decisions in life only after prayer and in agreement with your wives. And here is a final word: Paul says in Colossians 3:15:

> *And let the peace of God*
> *rule in your hearts....*

I have learned that if my spirit is not at peace when faced with a decision, I simply wait. When the decision is right, you will know—God's perfect peace will rule in you and your wive's spirit.

But, back to my story.

I accepted Pastor Ray Schoch's invitation, and for two years we pioneered Christian TV—this radical new concept of a whole TV station programmed 100% for the Lord. *What a challenge—like where do you get the programs?* Well, the answer was easy, you produce them, but the doing was next to impossible! Back in Rapid City it was a snap. NBC sent us 90% of our programming. All we had to do was a little news *(remember that one?)*, weather and sports. So who's going to do a Bible study…a children's show…a music program? We did have Pastor Schoch's Sunday services and what a great preacher he was. I learned more about raw faith from this precious saint than all of my previous schooling. Bible school teaches *about* faith—Pastor Ray *walked* it and *lived* it!

So, we went to work. Brother Willard Pierce, a precious elder on the staff, taught a daily Bible study, and how rich was his teaching. Believe it or not, I actually did my very first "Behind the Scenes" programs on Channel 30. It must have been my love for news born in Rapid City! Pat Robertson sent us the "Jim and Tammy" children's show. Remember that one? Jim Bakker, and his wife Tammy, pioneered a great children's program for several years.

Things were going great and Pastor Ray advised us that we should move up to Glendale, since I was driving fifty miles one way to work every day. We agreed and began a house search nearer to the church and TV offices. We also began having TV rallies, since our audience was growing and word was getting around that *CHRISTIAN TELEVISION* was on the air in southern California. By now we were actually on from about 5 p.m. to 10:00 p.m. Five hours a day was even a challenge, but everything was going and growing—even the finances were up dramatically—it seemed that your mother and I had finally found our place: a wonderful, spirit-filled church that owned a radio and TV station, with nowhere to go but up!

It was March 10, 1973—we had decided to invade

even Hollywood, California! For weeks we promoted it on radio and TV. We rented the Hollywood High School auditorium that seated about 1,000. We were so excited—oh how we hoped the partners would all turn out—and they did! It was glorious, the room was filled with enthusiastic, live wire, on fire, partners! The cream of the Christian crop—they had to be to have put up with some of the sorriest, poorly produced TV programs ever! They knew it, but loved us any way— we were pioneering 100% Christian television together! Doug Oldham was our special guest singer and speaker. He had recently recorded a hit Christian song that was sweeping the nation—"THE KING IS COMING"—remember that one? What a song and what a blessing it brought to the whole Body of Christ. We sang, shouted, shared testimonies, and praised the Lord. I shared the vision of not just one, but many TV stations—yes, a network to preach Christ from coast-to-coast. When we prayed the benediction and said good-night, your mother and I were glowing! Hundreds of wonderful partners had lingered to shake hands, greet us and congratulate us for the great new blessing of Christian television. Surely this was it— surely we were settled and secure in the ministry and calling that God had placed upon our lives. As we drove out of the parking lot of Hollywood High School that night we were higher than the proverbial kite...when God spoke! He spoke as clearly and distinctly as I had ever heard His voice. He said, *"Paul, I release you from your ministry at KHOF-TV."*

An atom-bomb going off at that moment would not have surprised me more! I was thunderstruck—for several moments I could not even speak! Finally, I turned to your mother and said, "Honey, you will never believe what God has just spoken to me!" Without a moment's hesitation she replied, "I know. God has just released you from your ministry here at KHOF." It took several more moments for the enormity of this immediate confirmation of God to register and settle in on me. Even at this earliest stage of what was, indeed, to become the final phase of our work and ministry, God had confirmed His word to your mother and me scripturally:

> *That in the mouth of two or*
> *three witnesses every word*
> *may be established.*
> Matthew 18:16

Not much else was spoken as we drove the hour or so back home. Like Mary, the mother of Jesus, we pondered in our hearts with awe the word of the Lord that had been spoken to us both simultaneously! In my mind the big question was—*"Now what? Why would God change anything that was going so well? Another TV station perhaps?"* We had longed for a station right in Los Angeles that would really cover all of the 12 million plus population of southern California. "Maybe that is it," I mused. But then I remembered that all of the TV stations allocated by the FCC were either on the air or under construction. Besides, I knew that the last sale of a TV station in this number two TV market had cost the buyer $1,650,000! How could your mother and I ever hope to raise that kind of money to buy a TV station?

For several days we interceded to God for direction. Finally, in prayer one day, the Lord reminded me of a fairly new TV station that had signed on the air about six months earlier. With fear and trepidation I finally phoned the owner, Bill Myers, to inquire on the status of Channel 46 which, by the way, was located on Mt. Wilson, next door to all the main TV stations for Los Angeles. I could hardly believe what I heard. He explained that his station had not been successful and that he had been forced to sign it *OFF THE AIR!* My heart did a few more flip-flops—I tried to sound only mildly interested as I made an appointment to discuss the possible acquisition of his station. The appointment was not for several days, so your mother and I continued to fast and pray for God's perfect direction and will.

A few nights later at the altar of our church, God began the molding process in our lives. You boys were there and may remember the unusual conclusion to that service. Your mother and I usually prayed together, but for whatever reason that night I knelt on one side of the church and she knelt on the other side. Unknown to either of us, at the time, we were both literally "slain in the spirit." We personally experienced those, *"...groanings which cannot be uttered." (Romans*

8:26) as the Holy Spirit made intercession through us. Suddenly, without warning, our pastor, Syvelle Phillips, moving by divine revelation, leaped to his feet and declared, *"A new television ministry is being born!"* It felt like a mighty bolt of electricity crackled through the air as wave after wave of glory swept through the room and into our very souls! We had told pastor Phillips nothing of our word from the Lord; he only knew that your mother and I were praying about some personal matter concerning our lives. We lingered at that altar till way past midnight, singing, weeping, and praising the Lord. Mark and Diana Yashuhara, the "Hawaiians," were there that night and their songs, anointed with the glory of the Lord, filled us with a wonder and sweetness I shall never forget. Here in only a few short days had come the THIRD confirmation of this divine call. At the conclusion of that glorious service, sweet little Grandmother Avery met me at the door as we were leaving. You wonder why we talk about and praise God for our grandmas? Let me tell you, if it were not for the *women*—and *especially* those grandmas—those *"mothers in Israel"*—there would be *NO* TBN! When we all get to heaven, we'll surely see that it was the "GRAMMAS"—Jan's group of *"GOD'S RADICAL ARMY OF MOUNTAIN MOVERS AGAINST SATAN,"* that have prayed us through every impossible situation! Grandma Avery reached for my hand and pressed a crumpled bill into it. Looking deep into my eyes, she said, "Paul, you'll need some finances to get started—

it's not much, but God will multiply it!" I hugged her and thanked her and later reflected that Grandma Avery's five dollar bill was the FIRST love gift that TBN would receive! Today, Grandma Avery is dancing on streets of gold, sharing in the nearly seven million souls that have received Christ through HER TBN!

Looking back twenty years, now, I can tell you, boys, this was IT—this was truly the beginning of HIS miracle! But, had we known the tortured trail that lay just ahead—well, that comes next. Let's move on.

CHAPTER 9

YE SHALL SAY TO THAT MOUNTAIN

Events were now moving at a dizzying speed as God began moving all the people, places, and things into place for the birth of His new television ministry. By now it was clear that our whole lives and direction were changing. With very mixed emotions I handed my resignation to Pastor Ray Schoch, who seemed very distressed by my decision. Why would I leave when all was going so well? Indeed, it seemed to everyone at Faith Center that we had just broken through, that Christian TV was finally over the hump and on the way! All I could tell Pastor Ray was that God had spoken—that He was calling me to a path unknown. With tears in his eyes, Pastor Ray finally spoke— "Paul, if God has spoken, you must obey. If you stayed, we would both be making a grave mistake and would be missing the will of God." Sadly, in the days that followed, many at Faith Center misunderstood our new calling. Harsh accusations were made that I was out to harm Faith Center—that I was deliberately seeking to start a competing TV station in the same market. I was even accused of stealing the TV mailing list which, by the way, I did not even have access to since it was held by a large mailing firm in Los Angeles. As I told you earlier, my sons, the wounds and hurts of your brothers and sisters are the worst spiritual pain you will ever feel. Your mother and I were devastated and nearly gave up in these early beginning stages of our new, and as yet unknown, journey.

One night in prayer with the pain of false accusations swirling all around us, God gave us a precious word of encouragement from Hebrews 11:8:

> *By faith Abraham, when he was*
> *called to go out into a place which he*
> *should after receive for an inheritance,*
> *obeyed; and he went out,*
> *not knowing whither he went.*

Your mother and I held on to that word and each other as we vowed to move on into the unknown.

A few days later we finally met with Mr. Myers and worked out a contract to purchase time on his TV station so that we could sign on right away. We agreed to continue working out the final purchase agreement for the entire TV station. In the meantime, $10,000 a month would pay for four hours a night and would enable him to sign KBSA-TV Channel 46 back on the air. With a hard gulp, I signed the contract!

About this same time God led us to a group of Christian businessmen who owned an industrial complex of buildings in Santa Ana. A computer firm had just moved out of 111 West Dyer Road—remember that address? Dear Lord, I will never forget it! Your mother and I still drive by occasionally and get goose bumps—you'll understand why as we move on.

Mr. Ward Vanguard, a member of our church, was one of the partners and had heard of our new venture through friends in the church. He explained that his building just might be a possible new home for the new TV station. As we walked through the empty rooms, I could hardly believe my eyes! Plenty of offices, large rooms with smaller glassed-in rooms for studios and control rooms, heavy electrical circuits and oversized air-conditioning for hot TV lights. God had designed it perfectly for a TV station! And, to clinch the deal, the owners gave us the first three months rent free!

On April 24, 1973, I signed another contract—this time a lease valued at over $250,000 with no guarantees or collateral of any kind. In retrospect, this transaction stands out as one of the great miracles that God did for us.

The ink was hardly dry on the paper, when I looked up and saw our car come roaring up to the front door of the leasing office. Your mother jumped out squealing, "Call Chicago in ten minutes...call Chicago in ten minutes!" When I finally got her calmed down, the story tumbled out. Somehow, news of our new station had reached Chicago and Mr. Jack Teas, a millionaire, who wanted to offer financial backing. I couldn't dial fast enough and sure enough, Mr. Teas answered. With only the briefest explanation, our new "benefactor" was actually on his way to California! When Mr. Teas arrived two days later, he looked more like Al Capone's bodyguard than the benevolent donor we had envisioned. For several days we discussed financing arrangements, loans, percentages of interest, collateral, and guarantees. At every lunch he always out-fumbled us and I picked up the check with our fast dwindling resources.

Here we learned a painful, but valuable lesson. My sons—do not depend upon the arm of the flesh! More importantly, we had forgotten to pray for God's direction or for the discerning of spirits which God gives us through His Holy Spirit. What followed was a total waste of our time and an even worse disruption of our work. We nearly lost our entire direction as Mr. Teas turned out to be full of hot air and provided no money! God had a perfect plan for His TV station and it did not include any phony millionaires! God wanted His little people, from the children to the grandmas, to have a part in his new TV station! Praise the Lord!

Now it was time to put some work with our faith. For days we scraped tile off the floors of the main studio rooms to make a smooth surface for cameras to roll on, hung lights, and hooked up equipment. So many wonderful volunteers with special talents began showing up. Everything and everyone we needed came and always just at the right time. A secretary arrived, carrying her own typewriter, a carpet layer just as the set needed carpet, carpenters, electricians, furniture movers—it was truly miraculous—God just sent them to us and always at precisely the right time as work progressed. One day we needed a gas line moved which was in the way of the lights that were being hung. We formed a little circle of prayer just as we had done so many times before. "Lord, we need a specialist for this job and we don't have the money to hire him...." The words were barely out of our mouth when through the door walked Bill Crandall. On his uniform was a patch which read, "Southern California Gas Company"! We laughed and cried and praised the Lord as Bill, tools and all, closed valves, cut pipe, and moved the line out of the way for the TV lights.

Finally, we were nearing SIGN ON! The final step was the microwave unit. This piece of equipment sent picture and sound from our nearly remodeled studio in Santa Ana to the transmitter on top of Mt. Wilson, almost fifty miles north. From there, the signal was rebroadcast to the vast southern California megalopolis. Again, a very specialized skill was needed. We began to pray—"Lord, where will we find a microwave engineer—who shall we call?" And as God is my witness, within minutes the phone rang. The caller? You guessed it—a microwave engineer! In a matter of hours he was there with four more engineers. They worked for three days trying to get the

TV signal from our studio to Mt. Wilson. Something seemed to be blocking the signal because nothing, not even a glimmer of the picture, was coming through. Maybe something was wrong with the equipment, after all the station had been off the air for over six months, so the engineers brought the receiver down from Mt. Wilson to the studio. They placed the transmitter a few feet from the receiver, turned on the power, and bingo! The picture was perfect. Nothing was wrong with the equipment. Finally, in desperation, we called the telephone company—they provided microwave services for many clients. The message caused our hearts to sink.

"Forget it!" was the word. They told us either the Whittier hills or possibly a part of Mt. Wilson, itself, was in the way. They had tried microwave shots from several spots in Santa Ana and it just couldn't be done!

Now we were desperate—we were running out of time—the FCC authority to remain off the air expired on Monday, May 28, 1973 and this was Saturday! The license could be lost if we did not meet the deadline and sign the station on that Monday! Once again, we had no one to turn to but the Lord.

I remember how discouraged everyone was. Again, it looked like we were finished. I really didn't know why, at the time, but I walked around to the back of the studio and began climbing the steel ladder to the roof where the microwave dish was installed.

I honestly do not remember that you boys were with me as I slowly inched my way to the roof. I guess I was in such a fog I was not aware of your being there. You will recall that just a few days ago, even as I was writing this account, you told me that you had both witnessed this amazing encounter with God. How thankful I am that you were there, not only to vouch for the truth of this miracle, but far more importantly, to know that there is a God in Heaven and that He really does move mountains! You both knew that we were at another standstill—another crisis—another test of our faith. NO PICTURE—and we had to be on the air within 48 hours! Tears began rolling down my face as I reached out and laid my hands on the cold curved steel of the microwave dish—"Father, you said that if we would have *faith even as a grain of mustard seed, you could SAY to THAT MOUNTAIN—be thou removed and be cast into the sea....'"* His holy presence descended upon the roof of that studio, and somehow I KNEW that my Heavenly Father had heard and answered my prayer. I dried my eyes and climbed back down the ladder. As I rounded the studio corner, I bumped into your mother who was crying and very discouraged. She asked where I had been. I explained that I had just had a talk with my Father up on the roof and that everything was going to be all right.

The engineers were very tired after twelve hours of hard labor, trying since early morning to get the TV signal through to Mt. Wilson. They were packing up to leave and everyone was very discouraged. I asked the chief engineer if they would all come back and try just one more time the next morning, which was Sunday.

Incidentally, this engineer had borrowed twenty dollars from me and was refusing to pay it back! He said, "Well, Mr. Crouch, it's your money."—(*how true*)— "We'll give it one more shot, but personally I think it's a waste of time!" I didn't tell him at the time, but the money was virtually exhausted.

The next morning, we were all there at 8:00 a.m. sharp. But this time something was different—there was electricity in the air! For several minutes circuits warmed up; transformers hummed; and final adjustments were made. The engineer up on Mt. Wilson was on the phone with the chief and all of us in the studio. Suddenly, a shout came from the telephone—we could hear it clear across the room! *"We've got it!"* he cried. *"We've got the picture and it's as clear as NBC!"*

All heaven broke loose in our little control room at 111 West Dyer Road in Santa Ana that Sunday morning! We laughed, we cried, we shouted! The engineers were thunderstruck—they could not believe what they were hearing. The chief was a chain smoker. He had kept the air blue with his smoke that whole week, testing the patience and sanctification of all of us. As he stared at the TV screen that Sunday morning, his cigarette dropped to the floor, he crushed it under his shoe and never smoked in that little studio building again. We all knew from that moment on we were standing on holy ground. By the way, he also reached into his pocket and paid back the twenty dollars that he owed me!

Yes, my sons, you are a witness. God moved a mountain for us and we will ever know that this was not just a spiritual mountain—this was a real dirt, rock, and tree mountain! Oh, praise the Lord! And for twenty years, now, the TBN signal has been passing through that "cleft in the rock" that our God carved for us. There really is NOTHING TOO HARD for our God! Yes, He made it possible for us to meet the FCC deadline in the nick of time! Yes, the miracle continued the very next night on Monday, May 28, 1973. Only three months from the time God first spoke to your mother and me, TRINITY BROADCASTING NETWORK was ON THE AIR lifting up Jesus with "LET'S JUST PRAISE THE LORD!" A TV station that had taken Bill Myers ten years to get permits through and build, by a miracle of God's will, was back on the air with 100% Christian programming in only three months!

That very first night we were on the air, telephone calls came in from all over southern California. How they even knew we were on is a mystery and a miracle all its own! Hundreds of God's wonderful people joined in just to "Praise the Lord" with us for this mighty new miracle of God. Many of the callers could not even see the picture since Channel 46 was a very low power station. Many said, "All we can see is a snow storm, but we can hear you just fine! Keep up the good work, we are praying for you!"

An interesting sidelight to all of the excitement of Channel 46 coming on the air occurred that next

Sunday at our church, First Assembly of Santa Ana. A fiery new evangelist from Texas had come to begin revival meetings. Dwight and Zonelle Thompson brought a whole new dimension to what we call PENTECOSTAL! Dwight was a refreshing infusion of new life to our *"California"* style of worship. The church was packed every night, but our new Christian TV channel was also on the air each night. The next Sunday morning, Sister Gertrude Pomeroy, one of the pillars of the church, came up to me and I could tell that something was wrong! "Paul Crouch," I knew when she called me by my full name—it was coming! "Why would you start your TV station right in the middle of Dwight Thompson's REVIVAL?" You see, she was torn—wanting to come to church, but also terribly excited by the new TV channel! I assured her that this dilemma would soon pass and finally appeased her by agreeing to come to her home to install a proper TV antenna so that she could get a clearer picture of Channel 46. We made our peace with Sister Pomeroy and she continued as one of our staunchest partners until her homegoing in 1992!

Yes, victory rang all across southern California that historic night that TBN signed on the air, and Dwight's revival was also a great blessing and success! But testing time was just ahead. *Buckle up*—there's a bad curve coming just up the road!

CHAPTER 10

YOU HAVE GIVEN ME NOTHING!

While time has proven that TBN was God's ultimate goal for your mother and me, and while it is now evident that most of our efforts and experiences were training and preparation for this goal, there was still a lot of *post-graduate* work that God had to take us through. Incidentally, that training is still going on in all of our lives.

My next great lesson was one I did not even know I needed. If you boys have not learned this lesson, you can save yourselves a lot of pain and sorrow by reading this chapter very carefully! Get a firm grip on your pocketbook, and then be prepared to turn it loose—let me explain.

We had agreed to pay Mr. Myers $10,000 a month for the four hours a day of air time, while still negotiating the purchase of the whole station. Your mother and I had invested our $20,000—*remember?* This represented our entire life savings. We had bought lumber for sets, paid the utility deposits, installed telephones, rented some TV equipment, plus paid Mr. Myers for the first few days of air time. Three days after the euphoria of signing on the air, our funds were nearly exhausted.

God had sent Jim and Tammy Bakker into our lives shortly before we had signed on the air. They had just recently left their work and ministry with Pat Robertson back in Portsmouth, Virginia. As I told you earlier, we had met Jim and Tammy back at Jim's home church in Muskegon, Michigan, never dreaming that our paths would cross again twelve years later in California. After much prayer and planning we had entered into a ministry partnership in this new venture—I was chairman of the board and Jim was president. They had arrived much like your mother and I had arrived in California—pulling a trailer with all their worldly possessions on board, and broke! While they had no money to invest, they brought something just as valuable—simple child-like faith in God, which was a source of strength and inspiration to us all. You boys will remember that you were dispossessed from your bedroom for a month or so as Jim and Tammy moved in with Tammy Sue and Biscuit, their tiny terrier pup.

Mr. Myers did not believe in credit, so he demanded an additional $3,000 before he would sign the station back on the air that third night! I recall turning to Jim that day and asking, "Now what?" Jim and I prayed for God's help and direction, when in the door came my pastor, Syvelle Phillips! We quickly explained our predicament to him and asked if he would intercede with Mr. Myers on our behalf. He did, and after a lengthy discussion and the payment of our very last $1,000, Mr. Myers agreed to sign the station on for one more night.

My emotions were so drained after that meeting, I knew it would be meaningless for me to try and face the TV cameras that night. Pastor Phillips said, "Paul, it is time to tell the people exactly what our need is." He agreed to host the program that night and I headed home to pray. As I drove toward home, I began to cry out my complaint to the Lord. "Why does it have to be so hard, Lord? Why do we have to suffer so much? Lord, you have provided everything we have needed up to this very moment—what does this all mean?" I literally pounded on the steering wheel of my car as I headed up MacArthur Boulevard toward home. As I wept before the Lord, that still, small voice spoke again—so sweetly and clearly this time that it startled me. The Lord said, *"Paul, it is difficult because you have not GIVEN me anything."* This message startled me even more! "What do you mean, Lord?" I protested! "I have given you everything—my ministry at KHOF and Faith Center, my life, my talents, EVEN our $20,000 life savings!" The Lord spoke again, and said, *"Son, you did not GIVE me your savings, you only LOANED them to me."* Ah, it was true! The Lord knows everything—even the secret thoughts of our hearts. I had taken a promissory note back for the money your mother and I had placed in the new ministry. We had only *LOANED* our money to God. Now, He said, "I want you to *GIVE ME* your savings!" Well, for me this was an awesome request. Didn't God know how *hard* your mother and I had worked for years to save this money? Didn't He know how we had sacrificed and even gone *without* to put this money aside for our future? But, without really realizing it, money had become a hindrance to my spiritual growth—perhaps even a *god* of sorts, and the Lord was asking me to give it up—ALL of it!

I struggled with the decision all the way home and finally as I literally fell across the bed, I said, "All right, Lord. I will make this bargain with you. If you will cause your people to give an equal amount—*TONIGHT, on television,* I vow to *GIVE* it *ALL* to you!"

In utter exhaustion, I picked up the telephone and called the station. By now, a full-fledged telethon was underway. Pastor Phillips and your mother were pouring out their hearts to the viewers telling of our vision and need at TBN. An unusual anointing of the Holy Spirit was upon Pastor Phillips as the opportunity for God's people to OWN their very own TV station poured from his spirit.

Somehow, I reached your mother who was also helping with the telephone prayer partners. I said, "Honey, God has spoken to me again." I told her what the word had been and also what I had promised the Lord. I said, "Tell Pastor Phillips that a pledge for $20,000 has come tonight from someone who loves Christian television very much, but ONLY if God's people will match it with an equal amount TONIGHT." There was a long pause on the other end of the phone as your mother began to weep softly. She knew better than anyone the battle that was raging within my very soul. My mind was in such turmoil by then, I really do not remember all that was said between us, but I do remember your mother's last word to me over the phone—"I love you, sweetheart"—and she was gone.

In a moment I watched, transfixed, as your mother slipped onto the TV studio set, tears streaming down her face, and handed Pastor Phillips the message. The challenge was given and the phones began to *ring and ring and ring!* All heaven came down as God's beautiful people began to call. In less than one hour they had not only matched the challenge, but there was a *$10,000 surplus!*

Yes, after only three nights on the air, on a station that had been dark for over six months—God spoke to his wonderful people to give over $50,000. And, since the need was so urgent, many actually drove down to the studio to personally deliver their gifts to THEIR TV STATION. All praise to HIS wonderful name! The "Red Sea" had parted and we were walking across on dry ground!

Without really realizing it at the time, I had put into motion one of God's most powerful laws—the law of giving and receiving—sowing and reaping. Years later, John Avanzini would explain and refine these powerful truths from the Word of God for all of us.

GIVE and it shall be given....

Now, my sons, here is the most valuable lesson that I learned and now pass on to you with all joy. From that night until now, neither your mother and I, nor TBN has *EVER* suffered an impossible need! I will ever know that our obedience to God that awesome night surely broke through some impenetrable spiritual barrier and has released God's glorious provision upon everything that we have attempted to do for HIM! Thirty, sixty, and one hundred-fold blessing is, indeed, a glorious truth and blessing for those who will simply obey the word of the Lord! Twenty years later I can testify to you that every bill is paid and TBN has ZERO capital debt! We literally, *"Owe no man anything, but to love one another...,"* as Paul admonished us in Romans 13:8.

One of the pledges that night came from a most blessed and unusual source. A missionary couple, Robin and Marva Farnsworth, had recently returned from New Guinea on furlough. They had been working for over eight years in the most primitive, disease, and mosquito infested jungles of the world as Bible translators with Wycliffe. The privation and physical pain they and their three children had suffered was clearly seen in their drawn faces. Brother

Farnsworth met me the next day at the door of TBN and said, "Paul, God has spoken to me and I must give you the balance of our travel fund for our new TV station." He held out a check with trembling hand. "God will supply our needs, I know; please take this with all our love."

My heart nearly burst within me as I looked at this thin, little man with the scars of physical and spiritual battle so evident upon him standing there before me asking to minister to my need. Tears welled up in my eyes as I opened the check—it was $1,480. "Oh, Brother Farnsworth, no," I cried, "I cannot take your travel funds!" As I spoke a look of intense physical pain came over his drawn face. He replied sternly, "Paul, *God* told me to do this. I must obey the Lord. You can't rob me of this blessing, you have to take it." With that he pressed the check into my hands.

My sons, if you have ever wondered why God is blessing TBN, look back at the precious seed which was planted by so many faithful servants of God like the Farnsworths. They so beautifully exemplify the word in Psalms 126:5, 6:

> *He that goeth forth weeping, bearing*
> *precious seed shall doubtless come*
> *again with rejoicing bringing his*
> *sheaves with him.*

This precious missionary family has proved this by their blessed example. Shortly after the miraculous birth of TBN, they returned to the jungles of New Guinea to continue their unsung task of translating the Holy Scriptures into the language of that needy nation. But, someday, they, too, will rejoice around the throne of God with the millions who have accepted Christ as Savior through this great voice called TBN!

CHAPTER 11

IN PERILS OF BRETHREN

The summer of 1973 moved by swiftly. These were busy months as Jim and Tammy, and your mother and I labored hard to establish what we prayed would be a solid foundation for the new TV station and ministry. But, as fall approached, it became very evident that trouble was on the horizon.

The key pastors of the area and church leaders really did not take our efforts too seriously at these early stages. Much to our disappointment we soon discovered, however, that many were not at all supportive of this radical new concept—a whole TV station devoted to 100% Christian programming. Your mother and I were so very naive in assuming that the Christian leaders would welcome this new tool for evangelism with open arms. There were, of course, notable exceptions. For example, our own pastor, Syvelle Phillips, and Pastor John Hinkle of Christ Church in Los Angeles; Pastor Leroy Saunders of North Hollywood Assembly of God; Pastor Dan Raculia of the Buena Park Community Church; Robert Schuller of Garden Grove Community Church; plus a few others. Thank God that the people, the Body of Christ, did open their hearts and even their pocketbooks, as I explained earlier; but the church leadership in general—well, that was another story. Their suspicion and ultimate rejection of our work was a source of great dismay and sorrow to all of us. I will always believe that the fear, which has now clearly turned out to be unfounded, was that television would be a powerful financial drain on the finances of the churches. For this, and perhaps other reasons, many churches and Christian leaders actually became hostile to this fledgling new ministry.

Jim and I were finally approached by several Christian leaders from the southern California region. Each of them had strong opinions on just how the TV station should be managed and operated. Some wanted, even requested, to be elected to the board of directors of TBN. Ralph Wilkerson, pastor of Melodyland Christian Center was one example. His church had just built a new mobile TV production truck and finally agreed to loan some of their equipment to us, in exchange for program time and a seat on the board of directors. We needed the equipment assistance so desperately that we agreed and voted to place Pastor Ralph on the board. Ultimately, he began to host some of the "Praise the Lord" programs and finally suggested that we move the whole station over to Melodyland Christian Center, arguing that this would save considerable rent money which, by now, we were paying to the owners of 111 W. Dyer Road. He was, in effect, suggesting that we make TBN an extension of Melodyland Christian Center. We knew this would be a mistake and we felt could actually harm the ministry if it were related to any one church exclusively.

Finally, my own pastor, Syvelle Phillips, feeling more and more left out of the progress and planning of the station, called Jim Bakker and me to a private meeting. His words were harsh and direct. He warned us that if we were to be associated with any church, it should be his—after all, your mother and I were members there and the real vision was actually birthed at the altars of First Assembly! He was also critical of some of the mini-fundraising telethons which we had conducted from time to time that summer, stating that we were asking too frequently for money. He also was not in agreement with some of the guests and musicians which we had been inviting to minister on the "Praise the Lord" program, which Jim and I had been alternately hosting. Finally, he exclaimed in conclusion, "You are running this ministry all wrong— you are heading it for the gutter!" We were stunned and devastated by this critical evaluation from one we had leaned on and respected so totally during the early birth pangs of TBN.

In an effort to appease the many voices that were overwhelming us, we finally agreed to enlarge our board of directors even more. Ward Vanguard, a member of First Assembly, was added at the suggestion of Pastor Phillips. Ralph Wilkerson also suggested a Christian attorney, Norman Juggert, that was doing much of Melodyland's legal work. Twenty years later, I can thank Ralph for this suggestion, since Norm has served faithfully and selflessly through thick and thin—mountain peaks and valleys—as secretary/treasurer for TBN. His staunch Lutheran-German roots have been a continual source of stability and wise counsel through the years.

As a result of this cacophony of voices and demands from many quarters, Jim Bakker and I, who had worked as a team in the early formative days of the ministry, began to grow further and further apart in the concept and goals of the ministry. Part of this distancing was basically a philosophical difference in several areas, but primarily in the financial area. Jim was much more the creative and artistic talent—I was the tightfisted, fiscal conservative. Jim wanted to build expensive and beautiful sets. He wanted to immediately begin buying time to syndicate the "Praise the Lord" program to secular TV stations across America. He invited friends and former associates from back east to join the staff and begin production on several new programs. Much of this was done without consulting the board or even myself, who was not only the chairman of the board, but also general manager of the business affairs of the TV station.

I recall one humorous incident on one of the mini-thons which Jim and I were conducting. Mr. Ward Vanguard, who you will remember, was one of the business partners who owned the building we were leasing and now also a board member, remarked on live TV—"Partners, please call and pledge for your new TV station. Our bank account is low and Jim Bakker thinks as long as there are blank checks in the book, he can just keep on writing them!" Jim was not at all amused and left the set hurt and annoyed.

Jim regularly complained to me that I was holding back the progress of TBN—that I should free him up to accelerate the growth and expansion of the ministry, but my pragmatic business senses told me we were heading for financial disaster if Jim was given full rein with no restrictions on him. As a result of the confusion and dissension that followed, God began to lift His blessing from our efforts and also our finances began to suffer.

My sons, we learned another important spiritual lesson at this point. Where there is contention and strife, the Holy Spirit is grieved and, as a gentle dove, simply withdraws the blessing and direction of the Lord. I must confess that Jim and I both lost our spiritual direction for a time. One day, in my office, Jim Bakker finally suggested that I leave the ministry. He offered to secure the financing to pay back the gift of $20,000 that Jan and I had given to get the station started. In the natural, I longed to accept his offer and get out while I still had some of my sanity left! But God would not release me, nor could I find any peace in the thought of leaving of the ministry that God had so clearly called your mother and me to.

Finally, it got down and dirty! At a board meeting, Jim asked to have several staff members admitted to speak some things that were *"upon their hearts."* I did not know it at the time, but Jim and Tammy had been having regular *"prayer meetings"* with several of the key staff members in their home. What all was prayed about, I shall probably never know, but it became clear as this agonizing board meeting progressed, that Jim had very cleverly and carefully orchestrated a *coup d'etat!* The production director, set builder, bookkeeper, and others testified to the board in session that it was Paul Crouch who was holding up the progress of the station and ministry. They recommended my removal and that Jim Bakker be made both president and chairman with full authority to run the operations of the station. I listened in stunned silence along with the rest of the board as witness after witness—probably about half of the staff—called for my removal. After the "kangaroo court" was ended, Ward Vanguard, the only seasoned businessman on the board, spoke first. Looking directly at me he said, "Paul, you are chairman of this board, and if I were you, I would FIRE Jim Bakker on the spot!" Jim's face turned pale and his character witnesses all beat a hasty retreat as the other board members unanimously agreed that I should remain in charge of the business affairs of TBN. Jim's *coup* had failed, but now the strained relationship between Jim and myself became virtually untenable. Division and dissension now reigned throughout the staff—those who supported Jim and those who supported me. We have seen this tragic situation occur again and again in church splits and we always wonder why—why must the Kingdom of God suffer such sorrow and indignity? After nearly 60 years on this earth, my sons, I believe I can answer that burning question, and I pray it will guide you and others through similar valleys of despair. Jim and Tammy, and your mother and I should have called a fast to bring all the staff together and we should have fallen on our faces before the Lord until we reached unity. God had a perfect plan and solution to our problem—He could have led us through every situation to total unity and victory—but we did not do this. I will always wonder—even twenty years later, if it was not God's perfect plan for Jim Bakker to lead the creative, artistic, and programming wing of the ministry and I, the business and technical wing. Some years later at a dedication service for Jim's new TV facility back in Charlotte, North Carolina, Jim said to me, "Paul, don't you see it now? God divided us that He might multiply us!" At the time this sounded right as TBN and Jim's new PTL Club were both prospering. But, now, with all that we know today—seeing the tragic collapse of PTL and Heritage USA, I still wonder if God's first plan was not His best.

Jim and Tammy's private prayer meetings continued

with their half of the staff. It finally became clear that Jim was planning an exodus to begin a separate new TV ministry in southern California. Your mother and I felt hopeless, helpless, and depressed. *"Where,"* we thought, *"do we go from here?"*

CHAPTER 12

CHANNEL 40 — HALLELUJAH!

There followed a time in our lives so dark and filled with such despair that it is painful to even think about it or to recall it in any way. I do not fully understand why it is that those whom we love the most, at times, are the very ones who hurt us the most. I do, however, have a partial answer, my sons. When at any stage of our lives we are not willing to totally submit our wills to the will of God, I can assure you, trouble will always follow. I have missed God's will many times and always lived to regret it. Remember my earlier lesson about finding the will of God? Tragically, Jim nor I, had allowed that *"PEACE OF GOD"* to *"RULE"* in our hearts.

The only reason I tell you of this time of testing and

despair is to let you know that even in the *"Valley of the shadow of death,"* our God is still there! We learned by personal experiences the cry of the Psalmist David:

> *Whither shall I go from thy spirit? or*
> *whither shall I flee from thy presence?*
> *If I ascend into heaven thou art there:*
> *if I make my bed in hell, behold,*
> *thou art there.*
> *Psalms 139:7, 8*

One night in the midst of our pain and despair, the Lord awakened me and it seemed I heard Heaven's choir singing that familiar old hymn, *"OH LOVE THAT WILL NOT LET ME GO."* Yes, God does give us songs in the night and He will not: *"Suffer you to be tempted above that ye are able; but will with the temptation also make a way of escape, that ye may be able to bear it."* *(I Corinthians 10:13)*

I also began to observe an ominous change in my usually bubbly and effervescent sweetheart, your mother. She began to withdraw into a melancholy state which was strange and frightening to me. For days she would sit in our bedroom without dressing or eating. You boys will remember this time most painfully. Your mother has given her full testimony of this nightmare which for months none of us could pull her out of. She could simply not function as a wife or a mother. You

boys had to literally learn to cook and wash clothes—
we all three had to fend for ourselves as your mother
sank ever deeper into complete depression. In her later
testimony she told of how Satan would torment her
with visions of herself—locked in some padded cell,
rocking and weeping—her mind gone. Finally, the
satanic temptation reached the point where she actually
planned to walk down to the Pacific Ocean beach,
about a mile from our home, and just keep walking—
out, out, out, into the cold dark water. Hopefully
everyone would think it was a tragic accident so as not
to bring the added shame and sorrow of a suicide upon
the family and TBN.

Now the ministry began to falter and stagger even
more as Satan hurled attack after attack at the very
heart of the ministry.

My sons, we have learned that this stripping and
emptying process is essential in every life that commits
wholly to follow the Lord. We have also learned that it
most always occurs just before God begins to thrust a
life or a talent into His full service. Months later,
Norm Juggert, my fellow TBN board member, put this
time of testing into proper perspective. He wrote a
note to your mother and me which said in part: *"The
Lord has laid it upon my heart to acknowledge the
great spiritual growth I have witnessed in your life
these past two years. I know, now, that the trials we
have experienced were not without purpose. The
success of TBN would have provided an almost
irresistible inducement for pride, had it not been for the*

trials that God used to temper and forge character and humility." Norm continues to be a strong source of wise counsel and advice.

The final blow came in August of 1973. The transmitter of Channel 46 up on Mt. Wilson suffered a serious fire in the antenna. We were off the air for several days. When the engineers finally got us back on the air, the picture which was weak and under-powered before, was now virtually unviewable. Many parts of southern California could get neither picture or sound. It looked like the end had finally come.

During all this time we had continued to negotiate with Mr. Myers for the purchase of his TV station, but were far short of our goal for the large down payment that would be required. Sensing that TBN would not be able to perform under the terms of our preliminary purchase agreement, Mr. Myers began dealing with other potential buyers for the purchase of his station. We finally learned to our utter devastation and dismay that a deal had been struck with Ken Connolly, a local pastor, and that within thirty days we would have to give up our programming on the station. Our *"christian brother"* had literally bought the station out from under us!

I remember walking into my office that next morning with my heart and hopes dashed again! Tears began to flow as I cried out to God for an answer—and again that still small voice spoke: *"Call Mr. Angel Lerma at Channel 40,"* came the word. "But Lord," I protested, "I called last summer, that station is not for sale." God's voice was unmistakable—"CALL!" I immediately obeyed the Lord and called. To my utter astonishment, Mr. Angel Lerma, himself, answered the phone. I learned later that this was *THE DAY* he had made his decision to sell Channel 40!

The very next morning I was in Mr. Lerma's office in Los Angeles. His mix of Spanish and English programming had not been successful and he was anxious to sell. The price—*one million dollars;* but the good news—he was willing to finance the bulk of the purchase price with only ten percent down or $100,000. For once in my life I did not even haggle over the purchase price. This time we signed our purchase agreement in advance of our going on the air. We were much wiser in our business dealings from that time onward.

Just prior to this new opportunity to acquire Channel 40, God had sent Paul and Joyce Toberty into our lives and into our TBN family. Paul was a successful contractor and an international director of the Full Gospel Businessmen's Fellowship. Paul agreed to join our board of directors as vice president. Not only did he and Joyce bring spiritual encouragement, but valuable business experience and financial guarantees as well. In fact, Paul and I, along with our wives, had signed personal guarantees to Mr. Angel Lerma, the seller of Channel 40, pledging to make the $9,044 monthly payments on the station if TBN was ever unable to make them! I remember the strange, almost frightening feeling as we signed the large, very legal looking documents. Our lives and now even our homes, in fact, all of our assets were on the line for Christian television. And yet, there was a feeling of joy, even an exhilaration—sort of a *"Here we go, Lord—we are in your hands!"* We also signed a concurrent air time contract which permitted us to continue our four hours a day of Christian TV programming without a break. In fact, we broadcast for several days on both Channel 46 and Channel 40, which gave us the opportunity to tell our partners of the change in channels. Praise God, in only two weeks we were *ON THE AIR on Channel 40* with four times the power and double the population coverage. What seemed to be the greatest tragedy, turned out to be one of the greatest blessings of all!

But, more trouble loomed on the horizon.

Jim Bakker, realizing the vast new potential of this more powerful Channel 40, made one last attempt to wrest control of the ministry away from your mother and me. For several days and countless board sessions, the various members and other spiritual advisors tried vainly to reason with Jim—hoping to yet reach an accommodation for a working relationship between Jim and myself. I was willing to try, but Jim was not. Finally, in anger, Jim stalked out of the meeting, cleaned out his desk and office, and left the building without even a word of farewell. In the absence of a written resignation, the board had no choice but to remove him as an officer and director, asking me to serve as the new president of Trinity Broadcasting Network in addition to my duties as chairman of the board.

CHANNEL 40 — HALLELUJAH!

In a matter of days we learned that Jim had, indeed, formed a new ministry which he called the Dove Broadcasting Network. About half of the TBN staff had left with Jim and efforts began in earnest to acquire a building and purchase air time on another TV station. Your mother and I were devastated, once again, to see such dissension and strife which was even boiling over into the partners of the ministry who were now torn as to whom they should support. Rumors flew thick and fast. We heard that Jim had acquired a large building just a few blocks up the road from TBN and that he was securing time on Channel 46 which had been purchased by Pastor Kenneth Connolly. But after about two months of desperate efforts to launch another TV ministry, we learned that Jim and Tammy Bakker had returned to Charlotte, North Carolina, where they did succeed in forming a new TV ministry which became Heritage USA and the rest is well-known history. One postscript which I must add to Jim and Tammy's credit came about a year after they had left southern California. One afternoon, our home phone rang and it was Jim and Tammy on the other end. Jim said, "Paul and Jan, Tammy and I are calling to say how sorry we are for the way things ended out in California. We feel...," Jim's voice paused, as he searched for the right words. "What I'm trying to say is that we feel that God cannot bless us back here in Charlotte because we have held bitterness in our hearts toward you and Jan." Another long pause. "We are calling to ask you to forgive us for anything we may have done to hurt you or the work of TBN." Your mother and I were overjoyed to accept this heartfelt apology and assured them of our unconditional forgiveness and, at the same time, asked them to forgive us for anything we might have done to hurt or injure them in any way. We concluded the call in prayer, wishing each other God's best in our future mutual endeavors.

It is interesting to note, my sons, that soon after that call of reconciliation, both ministries began to prosper in new and unusual ways. May we always remember that God cannot bless and prosper any one or any ministry where there is bitterness, strife, and unforgiveness. Learn this lesson early in life and it will be one of the important keys to your own success and future ministries.

As things began returning to normal at TBN, a most wonderful healing began in your mother. You boys remember all too well the long dark valley she suffered for many months during the horrible birth pangs of TBN. Finally, one Sunday morning, I insisted that she get dressed and go to church with us. I remember even having to help her get up and get ready to go. As your mother has testified many times, she cannot even remember the service, but at the conclusion she was captivated by a pitiful young girl who had timidly slipped forward at the conclusion of the service and was kneeling all alone at the altar. Suddenly, and for the first time in months, your mother received a word from the Lord—"You are to go and minister to that young lady." "But Lord," she protested, "I am the one who needs to be ministered to!" It seemed that no one even noticed this pitiful soul in tattered clothing and unkempt straggly hair. Finally, the Holy Spirit's urging prevailed, and your mother found herself kneeling beside this stranger that had wandered into First Assembly that Sunday morning. Out of a wounded little soul poured a story of sorrow and abuse that, as your mother said, "made even my trials seem small and insignificant." Tears flowed as confession was made and then the greatest miracle of all, a *NEW BIRTH in Christ!* You see, without even realizing it at the time, your mother had put into motion one of God's great spiritual laws—*you have to give the very thing that you, yourself, need!* A few nights later I was startled out of my wits as your mother sat straight up in bed at about 3:00 a.m. *laughing*—yes, *laughing* for the first time in months! The dream tumbled out between laughter and tears—she had been walking, she said, along a sea shore. As she walked she could see in the distance a group of men sitting around a campfire. As she drew even closer it was evident from the look of the ancient boats and fishing nets that this was long ago—Bible times! Finally, she saw *HIM!* It was *JESUS*—no doubt about it—so the other men were surely His disciples. As they were talking and eating, someone must have said something very funny and Jesus began to laugh! His laugh was so hearty that He leaned all the way back in an infectious laugh that spread to all the other men. With that—*snap*—your mother was awake two thousand years later, laughing with—*none other than Jesus!* Your mother's healing was complete a short time later when we made our first trip to Israel. As the bus drove along the shore of the beautiful Sea of Galilee, she shouted, "STOP! This is the place—I have been here before!" *DÉJÀ VU—that dream—Jesus and His disciples*—yes, it was there that Jesus healed my Jan, your mom, with a laugh!

CHAPTER 13

THE AGREEMENT IS ILLEGAL

During the early months of 1974, God's spirit began moving in a beautiful and spontaneous new way. Phone calls increased dramatically as hundreds called to accept Christ as Savior—*on LIVE TV!* Word of this new television ministry began to spread like wildfire all across southern California. Wonder of wonders, God was doing an exciting, *NEW* thing through a media that had heretofore been dominated by the world—*television!*

Melodyland Christian Center and Pastor Ralph Wilkerson had helped us through these early stages of development with much needed TV cameras and other equipment. While Ralph and I had strong philosophical disagreement on the future and direction of TBN, I will ever be grateful for his vision in assisting us during these early pioneering efforts. The problem was—"He who has the cameras makes the rules." If we made decisions (particularly programming) that were in agreement with Pastor Ralph, the cameras stayed—if we didn't, it seemed the cameras were needed at the church. Several nights we were simply off the air because the cameras were gone! Pastor Jerry Barnard of San Diego recalled at least one wild goose chase, driving the 90 miles up to Santa Ana, only to be told that cameras had been pulled at the last minute! Occasionally, ONE CAMERA would be left—a small, home quality Sony, which forced us to invent some rather innovative new production techniques! You boys should remember at least one night in particular. Paul, Jr., you were the director, and Matt, you were operating camera with the help of a box to make you tall enough! The trick was getting from the interview set over to the singers without a switcher. The problem was solved with a simple black card. When the host introduced the music, the card was placed over the lens of the camera. Quickly, the camera panned over to the music set and the black card was removed—presto—music and all without a glitch!

Pastor Ralph Wilkerson became increasingly unhappy as his efforts to move the entire TV operations to his church met with continued opposition from the board, and myself, in particular.

Finally, without any real explanation for his request, Ralph urged that Ward Vanguard be removed from the board of directors. I was devastated, since Ward had been a staunch supporter of your mother and me throughout the whole Jim Bakker affair, and had also voted to keep TBN independent of any one church, which I knew was mandatory if we were to serve all of the churches and Body of Christ. At the time, I could only conclude that this move was to gain more control of the board of directors. I tried to reason with Ralph, but he was adamant—Ward had to go—he insisted that I call a meeting of the board to remove him! When I broke the news to Ward, he was incensed. He reminded me of the considerable investment of time, and even finances, that he had placed in TBN during the first year of operations. After all, he and his business partners had furnished the building and studio that we were beaming the program from—and did I remember they had given us the first three months rent free? I sympathized and agreed, but reminded Ward that we were indebted to Melodyland Christian Center for the use of their cameras. Ward fumed that the church was being amply compensated by the free air time they were receiving for their church program, as well as the exposure they received each time Ralph hosted the "Praise the Lord" program. Finally, Ward Vanguard looked at me with eyes flashing and said, "Paul, I have no quarrel with you, but if Ralph insists on removing me from the board of TBN, I will have no recourse but to sue him and TBN!" Fear filled my heart at these words and I pled with Ward to reconsider. I reminded him that TBN was still in its infancy—that litigation would probably sink us! We had no resources—how would we even be able to afford to pay for legal defense? All reasoning was fruitless—Ward was furious—his parting words were, "I'll see you and Ralph in court!" Once again, I was devastated. With all the other agonies we had endured, how would we handle this one? A few days later, and to my surprise, Ward tendered his resignation rather than be removed from the board, but still vowed to see us all in court! It was Friday as I drove home to break the news of our latest impending disaster to your mother. The next day, an urgent call came through to our home—"Ward Vanguard has been rushed to Hoag Hospital in Newport Beach—he is in intensive care—please pray!" The next day, which was Sunday, was the first day visitors were even permitted. The doctor said I could only stay a few minutes. He also confided that the illness was a mystery—they couldn't seem to even diagnose what the problem was. As I entered the intensive care room, I was shocked and saddened. Machines and tubes were connected to Ward, it seemed, everywhere. A respirator was breathing for him—he was totally unconscious and probably unaware of my presence. All I could do was offer a brief prayer before being ushered out of the room. I learned, to my sorrow and dismay, that Ward Vanguard, my faithful supporter and friend, had passed away early Monday morning.

With a heavy heart, all I could do was commit this devastating circumstance and my brother Ward Vanguard to the Lord.

This was the summer of 1974, and we had finally completed and filed our application with the Federal

Communications Commission for the purchase of Channel 40. Now came the agonizing wait to see if our application would be approved. We had been on the air for almost one year; purchasing time first on Channel 46 and now on Channel 40. We were finally on the homestretch—we would know in about 90 days if God's people would finally OWN their very own 100% Christian TV station. Ralph Wilkerson knew that the continued assistance of his church was essential since we were, as yet, unable to purchase TV cameras and equipment of our own. So, as a final condition for the equipment assistance, Ralph asked that, at a minimum, his church board be given absolute control over the board of TBN. With Jim Bakker gone, and Ward Vanguard dead, the board of TBN was down to Ralph Wilkerson, Paul Toberty, Norm Juggert, and me. Paul, Norm, and I, were all in agreement that this was not the best decision, but what could we do? Cameras cost $50,000 each, not to mention the many other pieces of equipment necessary to produce TV programs. We searched and called everywhere, but to no avail. Finally, with no alternative, we agreed to Ralph's conditions. For three days, four attorneys and two certified public accountants, along with the combined boards of directors of Melodyland and TBN, hammered out the contracts. TBN would remain a separate corporation, but the Melodyland board, which Ralph was chairman of, would have veto power and control over all the affairs of TBN. I remember the uneasy feeling in the pit of my stomach as I, along with the rest of the TBN board, signed the voluminous multi-sectioned contract. The ink had hardly dried on the documents, until it became all too apparent that our new *"partners"* had very different goals and ideas for the direction of TBN. Demands and directives were issued which came into conflict with the many promises we had made to the partners and supporters of TBN. Your mother and I found ourselves in another bitter struggle for TBN's independence. God taught me one of the bitterest lessons of all in this college of *"hard knocks."* Day after day, and night after night, we agonized in prayer. There were times when I could not pray. The heavens were brass—God seemed so far away. We tried to extract ourselves from this agreement we had signed in return for equipment and technical assistance, but it had been drawn up by four top attorneys and two CPA's—*we had sold our birthright!* In addition to the agony of losing our position and ministry, we felt as though we had failed God and the partners who had worked so hard with us to bring it thus far. The blackness and bitterness were more than we could bear.

A few days later my phone rang. Norm Juggert, my fellow TBN board member and attorney, was on the other end. "Paul," he said, "I just may have some good news for you." My heart leaped for the millionth time! "The agreement we all signed with Melodyland...," he paused for a moment, "I think may be invalid because it seems to be in conflict with certain provisions of the California Corporations Code...what I mean is, I believe the whole agreement is illegal." For several moments I was speechless—could this be the release we had prayed for so earnestly. "I need to do some more research on this to be certain," Norm continued. "I'll be in touch with you shortly." As I hung up the phone my mind was in a whirl.

Suddenly, a memory flashback exploded in my mind. I remembered a strange encounter I had experienced on the very day we had signed this fateful agreement. Back in my office an unusual lady had asked to see me in private. She was elegantly dressed—in her early to middle fifties; but there was something very different in her appearance and mannerism. She had a most penetrating look—almost a fire in her eyes and she seemed to be able to see into my very soul! I had never met this woman before, but she knew my name. "Paul," she said sternly, "I have a message for you from the Lord." As she spoke she opened her Bible and read from a passage in Isaiah:

> *You have made a covenant with*
> *death...but your covenant...shall be*
> *cancelled and your agreement...*
> *shall not stand.*
> *Isaiah 28:15, 18*

With hardly another word she closed her Bible, stood up and left my office. I can now say that twenty years later, I have not seen nor heard from this woman again.

I remembered how strange and uneasy I had felt—

"Dear God," I thought, *"even if this message is from you, what can I do?"* The agreement was signed, sealed, and delivered. I argued within myself that there was nothing I could do about it now.

The memory of this meeting and my strange visitor passed like a flash through my mind as Norm's final words rang in my ears—"The whole agreement is illegal." A few days later, Norm's research confirmed the fact that our agreement was, indeed, illegal! God had blinded the eyes of four attorneys, two CPA's, plus the combined boards of Melodyland and TBN, to the illegality of this agreement which was not God's will for *HIS* TV station. *We were free!* Free to keep our promise that Channel 40 would ever and always belong to all of God's people; free to allow all the ministries and churches to be a part; free to depend on God alone.

Yes, my sons, God taught me one of the bitterest lessons of all, and chastened me most severely. By His grace and love, I have learned that lesson well.

The next Sunday night at First Assembly, where God had earlier and so beautifully confirmed our divine call, God gave us yet another powerful confirmation that we were back on track, and that He was moving us ever closer to the great purpose for our lives. Your mother's *Living Bible* fell open to Corinthians 8:10, 11 which read:

> *I want to suggest that you finish what*
> *you started to do **a year ago**,*
> *for you were not only the first to*

propose the idea, but the first to begin doing something about it. Having started the ball rolling so enthusiastically you should carry this project through to completion just as gladly, giving whatever you can out of whatever you have. Let your enthusiastic idea at the start be equalled by your realistic action now.

It was Sunday, April 21, 1974, when God gave us this wonderful word of encouragement. When your mother checked our diary later that night, it was exactly *ONE YEAR TO THE DAY* that we had first walked into the studio of what would become TBN! We laughed and cried again, praising the Lord for this message of His faithfulness and love.

CHAPTER 14

A $35,000 LUTHERAN

But now, as a result of our invalid agreement with Melodyland Christian Center, Pastor Ralph withdrew the equipment assistance, and also asked to be released as guarantors on a lease of $137,000 for some TV equipment which TBN had been able to secure in its own name. Further, and to our surprise, a phone call came from one of the board members at Faith Center, the owners of Channel 30 TV. The board member advised me that Pastor Ralph was attempting to purchase Channel 30 which was now experiencing some financial difficulties. When I called James Gammon, our FCC attorney in Washington with this news, he was extremely concerned. It was obvious that Ralph was unaware of FCC rules which prohibit ownership in more than one station in the same market.

"Ralph must resign from the board of TBN immediately," he declared. Also, and most serious of all, Jim said, "It could deny the grant of your application for Channel 40 at the FCC!"

With that, I immediately called a board meeting which Ralph did not attend. The board of TBN did the only thing it could do—we removed him from the board, lest there be even the hint of a cloud upon our FCC application for the license of Channel 40 which was now nearing a decision by the FCC in Washington.

Ralph said later that we had acted improperly, and sought a reversal of this action by the board of TBN, but our action was both legally necessary and final. We were at last free of outside control. Now the board of TBN was down to three: Norm Juggert, Paul Toberty, and myself. But, we were also free of any financial guarantor as we approached a most important deadline for the purchase of Channel 40. One of the main qualifications for any FCC application is that of financial ability to both purchase and operate a TV station. You will recall that we had agreed to make a $100,000 down payment to Mr. Angel Lerma, the owner, and that he had agreed to finance the balance of the $1,000,000 purchase price over the next eight years.

We had worked very hard during the early months of 1974 to raise the $100,000. We had held several mini-thons and spoken of the need each night on the "Praise the Lord" program. We had contacted foundations and had called every "rich uncle" we could think of from coast-to-coast! As I have mused so often when telling this story—all we got that month was the largest telephone bill we had ever received!

Finally, things got desperate—we had a firm deadline to place our $100,000 down payment into the escrow account of our bank. That day had finally arrived! We had been successful in raising $65,000 toward the down payment, but were far short of our goal. We learned later, that there were other parties that had offered Mr. Lerma more money for his station and were hoping that we would default! Not only would we lose the purchase agreement and the whole station, but even our $65,000 would be forfeited under the terms of the agreement! Once again, it seemed that all was lost!

My sons, another great lesson was about to be learned. I have since asked the Lord why, it seems, that He always waits to the very last minute to save us? Why must we always be at the bank of the *"Red Sea"* with the *"Egyptians"* swooping down on our backside with no way of escape? The answer came later in my quiet time of prayer as I sincerely asked the Lord for an answer. He said, *"Son, it is so that when the victory comes—there is never any doubt who did it!"* My sons, these times of extreme testing are absolutely necessary, for without them, our flesh would be tempted to take the credit, pride would follow, and then, what does the Word say about that?

PRIDE GOETH BEFORE
DESTRUCTION....
Proverbs 16:18

No, I don't like these heart-seizure kinds of tests any more than you do and, by the way, you both have had a few of your own, but they are absolutely essential to our spiritual growth and maturity. By the way, they will get worse and even more frequent as you move deeper into spiritual warfare! But, ah—the *VICTORIES,* the *VICTORIES!*

Your mother and I shall never forget *THAT DAY*—a day that shall be enshrined in the history of TBN as, perhaps, the greatest miracle of all!

The mail that day was dismal—only a fraction of what was needed. The typical daily financial report from my secretary was as follows:

> *Paul: Unless the Lord performs a miracle, we will not have a payday on Friday. We are in the red ($371.64). I have held the following checks: Baker Equipment Rental, $103.91; A-1 Janitor Supply, $131.83; and Orange Coast Hardware, $261.88.*
>
> *P.S. However, today's deposit is $246.63.*

Your mother was in the prayer chapel, crying out to the Lord in tears—eyelashes gone, mascara streaking her cheeks! I was praying and pacing back and forth in my office—by now it was about 2:30 and the bank *closed* at 3:00! Some of the staff were cleaning out their desks—this was it—wonderful while it lasted, but now time to go home!

Suddenly my phone rang. My secretary said, "Paul, there is a man out here asking to see you." "SEND HIM IN!" I shouted. "SEND ANYONE IN THAT COMES FROM NOW ON!" I added. This time our miracle appeared in the form of a *Lutheran* brother: *Scotty Scotvold!* You boys have heard me tell this story many times, but I want it recorded so you don't forget it! You see, there was not only a great miracle here, but another important lesson that I had to learn. As I have said so often, if I were God, I would not have chosen a Lutheran! *Lutherans weren't even Pentecostal, were they?* Surely God should have chosen an Assemblies of God brother—even Church of God—I would have settled for Pentecostal Holiness, although in those days we didn't agree 100% with them either, especially since *"eyelashes"* are forbidden!

Oh, how deeply rooted our little pet traditions and doctrines. How unaware of these silly prejudices, most of us are. God wanted me to know that HIS BODY was a lot bigger than I had imagined it to be! He wanted me to know that TBN was to be a *bridge builder—a repairer of the breach—a healing balm within His church.* How hard do these lifelong prejudices die—these traditions so carefully taught within the many denominational factions called Christian! I can testify to you, my sons, that most of those hateful, hurtful divisions, died within me, as this slight of stature stranger stood before me that day.

Finally he spoke: "Paul," he said, "I have been so blessed by your TV programs, and for God's people to have their very own TV station is almost too good to be true." I was wishing he would hurry because it was now about 2:45—the bank closed in fifteen minutes! Scotty continued, "I was on my way to buy a yacht, when God spoke to me." *"What? Does God speak to Lutherans?"* I thought. My prejudices were beginning to die, but they were not dead yet.

With that he reached into his coat pocket and, with trembling hand, held out a folded piece of paper that appeared to be—*could it be—A CHECK?* My heart was bursting as I quickly unfolded it—*yes a check and, as God is my witness, it was exactly $35,000!* My eyes filled with tears as I literally raced for the door! I'm sure at the time, Scotty must have wondered if I had lost my senses! I didn't even say thank you—*it was now ten minutes until 3:00!* Up the street I flew, breaking every speed law in this race with time. Fortunately, our bank was not far, but I distinctly remember looking at the clock as I burst through the doors of United California Bank of Santa Ana—*it was five minutes until 3:00!* I rushed to the escrow office and triumphantly laid the check on the officer's desk, directing that it be dated and placed immediately into our Channel 40 escrow account. I also called Angel Lerma, the owner, to let him know his $100,000 down payment was IN THE BANK!

When I returned to my office, Scotty was gone, but your mother and the staff were rejoicing! Later, of course, over and over with tears I thanked precious Scotty Scotvold, my *NEW LUTHERAN BROTHER,* for hearing God's voice, but even more importantly for obeying God's voice which had literally, and at the very last moment, saved Channel 40 for all of God's people. *Praise the Lord—the pillar of cloud and fire were still leading His simple, little children!* Our joy overflowed that night on the "Praise the Lord" program as we told of God's miraculous intervention once again to save HIS TV station and ministry.

As of this writing, Scotty and his dear wife Lucille, are still faithful partners of TBN, which has grown from one station, to 345 TV stations and is still growing! Scotty—the Body of Christ salutes you for your selfless obedience to the voice of God.

You know—I never did ask if he ever got his yacht!

CHAPTER 15

$137,000 IN BAD CHECKS

For days, the euphoria of our great miracle lingered. But, one great final hurdle remained before we would see the final victory and before we would finally claim the TV station that it seemed we had already given our life's blood for. We had leased $137,000 worth of TV equipment with which we were producing the "Praise the Lord" program, plus a few other programs that we were still purchasing time for on Channel 40. Melodyland Christian Center and Pastor Ralph Wilkerson had asked to be released from the financial guarantee which they had provided on this lease, as I have already explained.

I think you boys already know that even though Pastor Wilkerson and I had very strong differences on the future of Christian TV, and that those differences boiled over into many areas of the Body of Christ, the final chapter of our relationship with Melodyland and Pastor Ralph does have a happy ending.

Parenthetically, you will remember the many intense discussions your mother and I had concerning our relationship and struggle with Pastor Ralph over the control and direction of TBN. Matt, you may remember the day our family was driving down the freeway—I think we had just come from one of our traumatic meetings with Pastor Ralph. Your mother and I, as usual, were discussing the sorry state of affairs between Melodyland and TBN. Of course, the central theme was Pastor Ralph and his various directives and demands for the future of TBN. It was always: "Ralph," this or "Ralph," that. Finally, you, Matt, about twelve years old at the time, raised up out of the back seat of our car where you had been playing with your brother, Paul Jr., and exclaimed— *"RALPH, RALPH, RALPH—all I ever hear is RALPH! Can't we ever talk about ANYTHING but RALPH?"* Yes, out of the mouth of babes comes wisdom! Your mother and I were racked with laughter and at the same time rebuked by your youthful, but penetrating wisdom which had, no doubt, come from the Holy Spirit Himself! I'm sure that if your mother and I, along with Ralph, had listened more closely to the voice of the Holy Spirit, we would have not had those "traumatic" encounters which I have detailed for you in this account.

Well, since Melodyland had asked to be removed as guarantors on the lease, the leasing company as well as the FCC, had to have some new proof that TBN could make it on our own. The payoff, as I have told you, was $137,000, and we simply didn't have it nor did we have another guarantor to co-sign with us. We had exhausted everything we had just to complete the down payment of $100,000. We seemed to be at a total impasse once again. Paul Toberty and I had shopped all over southern California trying to get new leases, even trying to get our current leasing company to rewrite them for TBN. But, in 1974 money was tight—TBN was new. We did not have a "track record," they said. They could not be sure that TBN could make the payments without a financial guarantor. We were desperate, once more!

Finally, one afternoon as Paul Toberty and I sat staring at each other in my office, a new light which I had not seen before, flashed in Paul's eyes. "Let's write the checks," he said. For a moment it did not even dawn on me what he meant. "Write what checks?" I asked. "The equipment lease payoff checks," Paul replied. *"You mean the whole $137,000?"* I asked. "Yes, let's write them by faith," was Paul's firm reply. There was a long pause as the possibility of it all sank in on me. "All right, call Harold, the bookkeeper," I replied. The whole idea was crazy to Harold. "All I know is you'll be writing $137,000 in bad checks," he laughed. Nevertheless, the order was given and the checks were written.

Paul and I called our small staff together that afternoon as we laid the checks on the altar before the Lord in our prayer chapel. We joined hearts and hands as we cried out to God for yet another miracle. *But, now what?* You can't cash checks without the actual funds on deposit to back them up.

As I drove home that afternoon, the Lord once more spoke to my spirit. *"Whose station is Channel 40?"* the Lord asked. "Yours and the people's," I replied. The Lord spoke again, *"Who has always helped you when you had a need?"* My answer came immediately. "Your people, Lord." By the time I reached home, the light of God's revelation was shining in my eyes and your mother knew something new was up! "We're going to have a Praise-a-Thon tonight!" I exclaimed.

Your mother and the Tobertys were all negative to the idea. "We just had our Spring Praise-a-Thon two months ago—it is too soon," they said. But, I knew that God had spoken. In fact, I had seen as it were, a vision as to just how we were to begin. I saw us all kneeling on the "Praise the Lord" set, humbling ourselves before God and man on live television! By now, your mother and I were back at the TV studio getting ready for the regular "Praise the Lord" program. We conferred with the Tobertys by phone. They shared a scripture in Exodus which they felt the Lord was quickening to them. The consensus seemed to be that we should "stand still, and see the salvation of the Lord." But, as we read the scripture together again, one verse exploded before us!

> *THE LORD SAID TO MOSES, 'QUIT PRAYING AND GET THE PEOPLE MOVING! FORWARD, MARCH!'*
> *Exodus 14:15 (Living Bible)*

$137,000 IN BAD CHECKS

"We'll be there as soon as we can," the Tobertys said. "Go ahead and get the Praise-a-Thon started!"

I am sure that the world, who happened to tune by Channel 40 that night, wondered what peculiar people were these who, kneeling on "LIVE TV," confessed to their God that they were helpless without Him—that they needed a miracle once again.

I once said to your mother, "If I ever do write a book, I think I should title it—*'AND THE PHONES RANG, AND RANG, AND RANG.'*" Yes, every time we had a crisis—every time we were at the "Red Sea" it was *GOD'S WONDERFUL PEOPLE* on the phone, again, saying "Go for it Paul and Jan—we are with you!"

This night was no different. *"Ten dollars from Covina...fifteen dollars from Sylmar...one hundred dollars from Los Angeles...twenty-five dollars from Tehachapi...,"* as your mother read the pledges. The checks which we had written by faith lay on the table before us as God made the heavenly deposit through his beautiful people. By the end of that first night, well over $40,000 had been pledged! Praise God, the heavenly manna was falling!

But, our faith was to be tested once again. On the next night, your mother received a very special call. The man said he was a Christian dentist and a partner of TBN. He gave his name and a pledge of $1,000! In those early days, this was an enormous pledge! He challenged other dentists and doctors to call and match his pledge. Again, the phones began to ring. The dentists were responding—up and up went the pledges!

Now, the doctors were calling, too. A $3,000 pledge from one; $5,000 from another. Our total was nearing our goal of $137,000. Finally our dentist *"partner"* called back and said, "STOP THE TELETHON." He said he would meet with us next Sunday for dinner and would bring a check to complete our goal of $137,000! But something did not witness with our spirits. The Holy Spirit, through His gift of a "word of knowledge" was warning us—we DID NOT STOP the Praise-a-Thon.

The next day, as we phoned to verify the pledges, we were devastated. Most of them were phony. We had been deceived to the tune of many thousands of dollars. Now what? How would we explain and tell the real partners of this treachery? Your mother and I prayed for wisdom and strength. I knew we had to be completely open and transparent with our partners, so tearfully the next night, we told the whole, sad story. We moved our total board back, but now, it was God's move once again.

The phones were silent as your mother and I poured out our hearts and told of how we had been so cruelly deceived—of how our spirits had been troubled and warned by the Holy Spirit. But now, once again, the phones began to ring! And they rang, and rang once more. Before the evening was over, God's true partners from all over southern California had replaced the phony pledges with true pledges. We were back on track, moving toward the final phase of God's great miracle for HIS TV station which, for the first time, would cover the whole of southern California—over twelve million souls that would soon have 100% Christian television. We had begun the Praise-a-Thon on Thursday and by Monday, we had reached our goal of $137,000. I called our attorney, Mr. James Gammon, in Washington to tell him the good news. He relayed the message to the FCC which moved our application into the final phase.

Thousands of God's people rejoiced with us! We had passed our final hurdle—the promised land was finally in view. We now knew we were on the homestretch for the license of Channel 40—God's people were about to claim *THEIR VERY OWN 100%* Christian TV station.

But, as God would have it, I received the news, not in Santa Ana, but in Chicago. I had travelled to the offices of the German-made Fernseh camera company to check out their latest equipment. In the middle of intense negotiations for new TV cameras, we were interrupted with this message—*"Have Paul Crouch call Mr. James Gammon in Washington—it is urgent!"*

CHAPTER 16

COMMISSION GRANTED!

We had filed our application for the license of Channel 40 in early May. Knowing that it takes the FCC about 90 days to process a fairly routine application, we knew that decision time was near. This application may have been routine for the Commission, but it surely was NOT for us! We had sweat blood and come through hell and high water to see THIS APPLICATION to its final stage.

When the call came to me, there in Chicago, I knew it had to be about our application, since it came from our FCC attorney, but I also knew the decision could be DENIED just as well as GRANTED! I asked the camera salesman if I could please use his telephone. As I dialed the number, my heart was racing! I had to sit down—cold sweat broke out on my forehead. I'm sure my hosts thought I was ill, or at least receiving some kind of tragic news. Mr. Gammon said, "Paul," an eternity passed between my name and the next word! "I have GOOD NEWS!" The bells of heaven rang! I heard the *"Hallelujah"* chorus! I shouted and then dropped the phone! Jim continued, "A telegram is on the way from the FCC—your license for Channel 40 has been **GRANTED!**"

As quickly as I could excuse myself, I headed for my hotel room! There, I threw myself across the bed as I wept my thanks and praise to God. It was there that the Lord gave me one of the most precious words I have ever received. As I do so often, I flipped my Bible open and this verse leaped off the page:

> *He hath delivered my soul in peace from*
> *the battle that was against me: for there*
> *were **many** with me.*
> *Psalms 55:18*

I rushed home—August 2, 1974—to await the call from Western Union that the telegram had arrived. Another eternity passed, but at about 3:00 p.m. the call came! As I roared out the driveway to personally pick up the telegram, your mother and Joshua (our big, white, german shepherd) were actually doing a *DANCE* out on the patio—I am sure it was in the Spirit! I could hear her clear down the street laughing and crying— "Josh, we got it!—Josh, we got it!"

We will never forget that night—*August 2, 1974,* as we read the telegram on "Praise the Lord"! Our joy overflowed as God's people from all over southern

California claimed THEIR TV STATION in Jesus name!

One of our partners, Loraine Napier, expressed perfectly the great joy we all felt flooding our souls:

> *Dearest Paul and Jan: Whoever heard tell of one on a welfare grant owning a TV station? Well, I do! My Heavenly Father bought me one tonight! P.T.L.— Fantastic! Imagine me, a financial nobody, suddenly part owner of not only the CATTLE on the hill, but the HILL itself! There's a chunk of Mt. Wilson up there tonight which actually belongs to us! Can you believe it? Talk about the unsearchable riches of God!*

Now the station was ours and the hard work began in earnest. Weeks of preparation in anticipation of this great day had already laid a good programming foundation. Your mother and Sally Holiday did a ladies' program called *"Happiness Is."* Pastor Ed Smith did a Bible study along with Dr. Robert Frost. Delbert Hosteller did a sign language program for the deaf; the Catholics did *"It's A Brand New Day";* and yes, I continued the second oldest program even to this date—"Behind the Scenes." Some of the programs had been planned, but not actually produced. But now we all rolled up our sleeves and began the joyful task of creating *CHRISTIAN TELEVISION* for *ALL* of southern California.

One small change in the programming brought me more personal satisfaction than just about any other. For months, as we had been purchasing the air time from Mr. Lerma, at the end of every "Praise the Lord" program the station ran a "disclaimer" which read: "The views expressed on the preceding program do not necessarily reflect the views of the staff and management of Channel 40 TV." The announcement had always grated on my nerves—especially on nights when we had seen a mighty move of the spirit of God. When we finally took possession of *OUR TV STATION,* I got my revenge! I changed the *DISCLAIMER* to what I called a *"CLAIMER"* which now read: *"The views expressed on the preceding program do MOST DEFINITELY express the views of the staff and management of Channel 40!"* We all got a chuckle from that one!

The next several months and even on into 1975 were happy, productive, and busy months. Our board, which still consisted of Norm Juggert, Paul Toberty, and myself, worked beautifully together as Channel 40 began to bloom! Paul, who was a general contractor and an excellent businessman, helped us make plans for our very own studio building just across the line from Santa Ana in Tustin, California. We were finally able to lease a one and a half acre lot in a new industrial development that was being built by the giant Irvine Company.

Paul also strongly recommended that we add a new board member, brother Demos Shakarian, well-known as the founder and president of the Full Gospel

Businessmen's Fellowship International. Paul had been an international director and chapter president for several years, and felt that brother Demos' presence on the board would add credibility and strength to TBN. I was not too enthusiastic at first—I had been hurt and stymied by differing goals and visions for TBN by several earlier board members, but Norm and I finally yielded to Paul's desire and welcomed brother Demos Shakarian as an official member of the board of directors for TBN. Demos brought even more valuable business experience to our work and for a time helped TBN immensely as we entered our first phase of rapid growth.

About this same time, the Lord began to deal with my heart concerning the breach of fellowship that I had personally suffered with Pastor Ralph Wilkerson. My sons, listen up—another lesson to be learned. Without really realizing it—or at least unwilling to admit it—I had carried a real root of bitterness toward Pastor Ralph. In my mind he had tried to take TBN away from your mother and me. I was convinced that if he ever did gain total control of TBN that your mother and I would be history! I am sure, now, that in Ralph's mind, he felt he was doing the very best thing for the good of TBN and the Kingdom of God. One day the Lord spoke very clearly and said: *"You are to call Pastor Ralph Wilkerson and ask him to forgive you."* The word not only startled me, but also displeased me! After all, didn't God know that it was Ralph that had hurt *ME!* I was the totally innocent, wounded party—I should have an apology from Ralph! But, as the Lord continued to deal with my heart, He reminded me of the scriptural command that if our brother offends us —we are to go to him (Matthew 18:15)—I was to take the initiative. Finally, I called—I asked Pastor Ralph if he would meet me for lunch. I am sure he wondered just what Paul Crouch wanted with this request for a luncheon meeting, but he readily agreed. Neither of us ate any lunch that day as I simply opened my heart to Ralph and confessed the bitterness I had held toward him through our trials and tribulations. It was one of the most difficult things that God had ever required me to do, but I finally said, "Ralph, will you forgive me?" Tears welled up in Ralph's eyes as he graciously accepted my apology, and then offered one of his own, as he asked me to forgive him for any perceived hurt or injury. Ralph and I have stood together many times, since, on the platform of Melodyland Christian Center. He has appeared on "Praise the Lord" and other programs. The wounds and sorrows of the past are healed as both ministries have moved on in building the Kingdom.

My sons, I am convinced that TBN would not have been successful had I not obeyed the Lord and asked for Ralph's forgiveness. Always remember the old adage: *"It is the little foxes that spoil the vine."*

Now things really began to explode at TBN. By mid-1975 our new studio building was fully underway. We would finally have a home of our own, so necessary if we were ever to have *24-HOUR A DAY* Christian television.

COMMISSION GRANTED!

I remember taking your Papa Bethany, your mother's dad, out to the bare piece of ground before construction had begun. Weeds were waist high as we walked the four corners of the property. Finally, he knelt down and with hands raised high he declared, "This shall be the WORLD HEADQUARTERS OF TRINITY BROADCASTING NETWORK! After prayer and praise, he picked up a small clump of dirt, folded it neatly in his handkerchief, and vowed to pray every day for TBN! What a saint, your Papa Bethany, and how we miss him and his prayers today.

But now, in addition to a new studio, other awesome opportunities began to present themselves. Mr. Gammon, our FCC attorney, called one day and advised me that UHF TV allocations were opening up in many major cities across America. As a result, we filed applications for Houston, Denver, and Seattle. In early 1976, an opportunity opened to purchase an existing station, Channel 21, in Phoenix, Arizona. Later, an application was filed for Oklahoma City. The story of each of these great stations could fill a book of their own as we went through many of the same trials and tribulations we had gone through with Channel 40!

I may never know for sure just why, but this flurry of activity and growth began to disturb Demos Shakarian, and since he and Paul Toberty were so closely related in the Full Gospel Businessmen's Fellowship, he too, began to question all of this rapid growth. Your mother and I became increasingly perplexed, along with Norm Juggert, as to why everyone was not just as excited as we were about the possibility of new growth and *more stations!* My sons, as I told you earlier, in retrospect I believe that much of the Christian leadership actually feared that Christian TV could become a serious drain on the overall finances of the churches and para-church organizations. I think the perception was, and may still be, that there is only a limited number of dollars out there and that TBN might cut the pie thinner for them. Time has surely disproved this as numerous new ministries and new mega-churches have arisen these past twenty years along with Christian television.

I do recall Demos saying on one occasion, "Paul, why do you have to pull so hard for finances on your telethons? You are pulling too hard for money!" I had never perceived that we were "pulling too hard"—most of the telethons were times of great refreshing and more like old time revival. It was true, however, that TBN's finances were going up at an awesome pace. We had finally hit pledges of a *MILLION DOLLARS* in the fall 1976 Praise-a-Thon!

Finally, at a board meeting I shall never forget, Demos looked at me sternly and said, "Paul, you will not build any more TV stations—ONE STATION is enough!"

Your mother and I were devastated once again and there ensued, my sons, another valley of testing and despair. And yet, in the end—well, here I go, getting ahead of my story again!

CHAPTER 17

AND I SAW ANOTHER ANGEL

Looking back these twenty years, it is amazing to see that in spite of changing board members, in spite of struggles for control, and in spite of conflicting ideas and goals for the ministry—TBN continued to *GROW* at an incredible pace. This was, and is, surely God's miracle that had, indeed, been confirmed by a beautiful word of prophecy given at one of our rallies in the early days of TBN. Jerry Barnard, pastor of Christian Faith Center in San Diego had given this most encouraging word of prophecy which was recorded on tape and later transcribed word for word:

> The Lord Himself would say unto you—
> the investment of time and money, the
> investments of life and blood itself that
> you have made for my cause has been
> noted by the Lord and has been taken

note of even in the record books of heaven. Fear not, neither seek the applause nor the praise of men for they will not always understand your vision. But believe and know that what I have willed, and what I have begun, no man can stop, and no man can detour, and no man can take away. For I the Lord will cause my work to prosper and grow, and there will be no storm, there will be no great power that will come against my will, that will overpower it. For I will accomplish the work that I have set forth to do. For I am the Lord and it is my work saith the Lord God Almighty.

The date was June 15, 1975.

A few months later, in October of 1975, I remember so clearly reflecting on the future of TBN in the den of our home. I knew in my spirit we would one day have a network of TV stations spanning the continent. We were already filing applications with the FCC to accomplish this in spite of board objections. But I did *not* expect, in my wildest dreams, the awesome revelation that came to me that Saturday afternoon! As I was praying and seeking the Lord for the future of TBN, that familiar voice spoke again! This time in the form of a vision so vivid and startling, I had to catch my breath. I saw on the ceiling of our den, a giant map of the United States. Hovering high above it was a bright light and issuing from it were beautiful streams of light moving toward the outline of the map. The streams of light then began to strike the major population centers: Los Angeles, Miami, New York, Seattle, and so on until the whole country was surrounded. As the streams of light landed, secondary lights were illuminated, and then, in extremely rapid succession, small thread-like streams of light began to spread out, and as they spread, little dots of light began to glow until the whole map was literally bathed in a network of lights! I sat there transfixed by what I was seeing as I cried out to God to show me what all this meant. As I waited upon the Lord, He spoke a ringing, resounding word to my spirit—*"SATELLITE!"* "But, how, Lord? When, Lord?" I began to cry. *"Soon,"* came the voice of the Lord. *"VERY SOON."* As the vision faded from my consciousness, only then did the enormity of it all begin to settle in upon me, filling my very spirit, soul, and body, with an excitement and anticipation I had never known before!

A few nights later God confirmed my vision through Pastor John Hinkle, pastor of Christ Church, in Los Angeles. John had been our guest on "Praise the Lord," as God began to move in mighty healing power. The prayer lines were literally jammed as calls came pouring in from all over southern California. *"Praise God, I'm healed of arthritis! I can move without pain!"…"My left ear just popped open—I have been deaf for fourteen years!"…"My tumor has just disappeared—right before my eyes!"* Before the

137

program ended, over *250* testimonies had been received, praising God for miraculous and instantaneous healings! But God was not through revealing His "word of knowledge" that night. As Pastor Hinkle drove home in the wee hours of the morning, the spirit of the Lord came so powerfully upon him, he told us later, that he had to pull his car to a stop off the freeway. God said, *"What you have seen tonight of my healing power, you can multiply ONE HUNDRED-FOLD! I will, indeed, raise up a mighty network with 100 stations across America!"*

Here, again, was God's mighty confirmation of His glorious plan—a gigantic Christian television network that would "give the winds a mighty voice!" Praise God, twenty years later, this word of the Lord has come to pass. As of early 1993, there are 345 TV and radio stations ON THE AIR worldwide. Of that number, over fifty are maximum, FULL POWER STATIONS. It would seem that God is not counting the smaller, low and medium power stations, but intends even yet, to give us those 100 FULL POWER TV stations before He returns in power and glory. My sons, with what I know now, when that 100th full power station signs ON THE AIR, I will be packing my bags for Glory! Surely that day is not far away!

Not long after this vision and several confirmations by other men and women of God, I was contacted by RCA Americom, the *satellite division* of the RCA corporation. They were preparing to launch their first television communications satellite so they called on us to see if TBN would be interested in acquiring a channel on SATCOM I to feed our TV signal to the growing number of cable stations, plus any other broadcast stations that we might acquire in the future! I remember, my heart skipped another beat when the contract was presented—$34,000 a month for a full 24-hour a day channel! *Dear Lord, our whole budget was less than that a month,* but by faith we signed it—committing to one whole channel on *"ANGEL I,"* as we called it, which was to be launched in the next few months.

Now, we would have to file for the most exciting FCC license of all—a SATELLITE TV station that would cover the whole north American continent! The industry was so new that the FCC did not even have any satellite application forms prepared as yet. But, we applied anyway! Our FCC attorney helped us, and with our engineer's input, we filed for the FIRST southern California satellite station. I'm sure you boys will remember the great excitement as we raised the funds in the fall of 1977 for this most awesome step of faith yet for TBN. Next, the huge ten meter dish was ordered plus all of the exotic electronics to go with it. Then came the wait, as usual, for the FCC to process our application. Days dragged into weeks, and weeks into months. Each time we would call our FCC attorney, the word was the same—"next month," then "next week," then "next Monday" and so on. For nearly six months this was the pattern. Finally, we were desperate. Every time I drove in and out of the parking lot, the huge pile of packing crates containing the satellite equipment would confront me. It seemed as though this mountain of equipment was mocking me. Thousands of dollars worth of equipment sitting there, ready to go…but no FCC authority to build. To make matters even worse, word came from our attorney, that the FCC might be reviewing this whole concept of satellite authorizations; it might be referred "upstairs" to the full Commission for action. That could take many more months—my heart sank within me.

"Dear Lord, another 'Red Sea'—another impossible situation," I thought. The final word from our attorney on Thursday morning, February 16, 1978 was, "Paul, I have no news…." The sick feeling in the pit of my stomach deepened. "Maybe next week—Tuesday or Wednesday," his voice tried to sound reassuring. At about 6:00 p.m. I went into my office, locked the door, and lay prostrate before the Lord. As I agonized in prayer, God showed me clearly what to do. Remember, my sons, God's promise:

> And ye shall seek me, and find me, when
> ye shall search for me
> with all your heart.
> Jeremiah 29:13

As I have said so often, God delights to allow these impossible situations to prove HIS mighty power to deliver!

The "Praise the Lord" program was live that night and your mother and I were hosting. Back then, it began at 9:00 p.m., so for nearly three hours I interceded for His direction. As I prayed, the Lord showed me that we should turn the whole "Praise the Lord" program into one gigantic prayer meeting. You see, He wanted all the TBN partners to be a part of His next great miracle! At 9:00 p.m. the familiar "Praise the Lord" theme echoed out across the airwaves. Your mother and I poured out our hearts and burden to the most wonderful partners in the world. The "PTL" chairs and table were moved back out of the way as we knelt before the Lord and began to pray. Thousands joined in as we sought the Lord with all our hearts. Jim and Carol Hampton were our guests that night along with Dr. Russell Spittler from Fuller Theological Seminary. What a glorious prayer meeting we had! Many other unannounced guests, including Jerry and Sandy Barnard, simply stopped by led to come that night by the Holy Spirit. At about 12 midnight, the burden lifted, we knew God had heard the cry of His children—we had, as the old timers say—*"PRAYED THROUGH!"* But, we never dreamed how quickly the answer would come. Oh we of "little faith"!

The very next day, Friday morning, an urgent call reached me. The operator advised—"WASHINGTON, D.C. calling." *"It can't be this soon,"* I thought. "Paul, I can't believe it, but...." The excitement in Jim Gammon's voice was unmistakable. "We have your construction permit from the FCC for your new satellite station!" "But, how?" I exclaimed. Jim replied, "I simply don't know, Paul, I have never experienced anything like this in all my legal career—it has to be God's miracle!" And for our FCC attorney that was quite a confession!

Joy flowed like a mighty river as we flashed the good news to our TBN partners the very next night. Another MIGHTY STATION was born! The answer had come in only *TWELVE* hours!

In days, the giant ten meter earth satellite dish was hoisted onto its foundation. Its gleaming white frame tilted at an unusually high angle, ready to probe the heavens in search of its target. The target: a wing-shaped package of highly sophisticated electronic wonders—22,000 miles above the equator in stationary orbit—yes, "ANGEL I" was flying high, and now—wonder of wonders—we could talk to it.

That night the Lord gave us a prophetic promise from His word:

> *Ask of me and I shall give thee*
> *the heathen for thine inheritance,*
> *and the uttermost parts of the earth*
> *for thy possession.*
> *Psalms 2:8*

Yes, God gave us HIS mighty *satellite angel* to reach our world with the Gospel of Christ. God knew that our generation would be the first generation to fulfill this glorious prophecy. As the Lord would have it, our first transmission would be an "earnest" of that inheritance. On April 10, 1978 at the National Association of Broadcasters Convention in Las Vegas,

Nevada, we sent our first full "Praise the Lord" program to all of the exhibitors. Hundreds of secular broadcasters from all over the nation received the Gospel—we were finally HEAVEN BOUND!

CHAPTER 18

NO MORE STATIONS

My sons, as I told you at the beginning of this account, the worst pain always seems to come from those you love the most. Surely this next chapter confirms that sad reality. Demos Shakarian was and still is today one of the giants of the faith! He has shared the miracle birth of the Full Gospel Businessmen's Fellowship International many times on TBN and, of course, in countless banquets, conventions, and books. Demos and his wife, Rose, are living legends as their great work has spread around the world. The testimony of Demos' calling from the Lord was just as miraculous as the call your mother and I had received, and we have always held him and the work of the Full Gospel Businessmen in highest esteem.

But, as I explained earlier, the explosive growth of TBN became a matter of great concern to Demos, as well as his close associate, Paul Toberty. I was determined to seize every opportunity to expand the ministry of TBN, so as applications were filed for more TV stations, we naturally had to expend TBN funds for attorney fees, engineering services, filing fees, plus the costs of forming new corporations. In those days, the FCC looked more favorably on your application if you applied through a corporation which was domiciled in the same state as the TV station. Thus, we formed Trinity of Arizona, Trinity of Florida, Trinity of New York, and so on.

Since Demos and Paul were fifty percent of the board, they had *de facto* veto power over myself and Norm Juggert. By the way, this was a very unhealthy combination—that is why most all institutions, from the Supreme Court all the way down to the smallest city council, have an odd number of members— otherwise similar deadlocks can occur.

Finally, at our next board meeting, I was ordered not to expend any more funds on these newly emerging corporations. I was told that it was improper to transfer funds from one corporation to another without board approval. To make matters even worse, members of the Full Gospel Businessmen in Oklahoma City, Houston, and Seattle, who had been very supportive at first, now refused to assist us in our efforts to acquire stations in those cities.

Your mother and I were frustrated again as we could see no way to move on with what we knew was the vision for TBN. Finally, in prayer, the idea of spinning the "Praise the Lord" program off into a separate department came to me. After all, this program was unquestionably the main driving force of the ministry, and the one I had been solely responsible for. Also, most of the funds coming into TBN were a result of the "Praise the Lord" program, so a special segregated fund was created for "Praise the Lord" which gave us the ability to pursue the dream of a television network that I knew would one day span the continent.

When this was discussed in a board meeting, Demos and Paul were not, at all, in agreement. In their minds, I was deliberately circumventing the authority of the board and they demanded, and then unilaterally ordered, an audit of the books by an outside certified public accounting firm. I felt this was a waste of much needed funds knowing that we had done nothing wrong and that all funds could be properly accounted for. Norm Juggert tried vainly to be the peacemaker and the mediator, but the sad truth was we were locked in disagreement, once again, for control of the future of TBN.

How sad that even within the Body of Christ, when confidence and trust is lost in each other, all kinds of tragic thoughts, feelings, and actions are the result. I truly believed that Demos and Paul were hoping that the audit would reveal some impropriety or illegal action so that they would have justification for removing me from the board. It was very wrong for me to have such thoughts, but when the flesh takes over, as it surely did here, all kinds of unholy fruit is manifest!

Demos and Paul selected the accounting firm and

for several days they poured over the books and records of TBN. They examined the daily deposits of donor mail, checked bank accounts, asked me many questions, and finally submitted their report.

What the report showed clearly was that funds had simply flowed through the "Praise the Lord" account and that all TBN bills had been paid as usual in a timely manner. It showed that we had, indeed, continued to expend funds for the growth and development of TBN, and that every penny had been spent in accordance with the IRS exempt purpose of the corporation. In fact, much of the funds had been expended for the expansion of TBN in accordance with the designation of the donors. This was only natural since we were asking our partners to give for specific new areas of outreach such as Phoenix, Oklahoma City, and Seattle. When the two TBN accounts were finally reconciled, there was a slight difference of about eleven dollars, which the auditors said was a simple bookkeeping error on our part.

When the report was read at our next board meeting, I honestly felt that disappointment was registered on Demos' and Paul's faces, but this was probably just my flesh reacting again. At this board meeting, however, we had a new attendee—*YOUR MOTHER!* While she was not an actual voting member of the board, she nevertheless demanded to be heard at this meeting. We learned later that most of the employees of TBN were *de facto* attendees at this board meeting, since your mother's voice was clearly

heard up and down the hall! The obstructionist tactics
of Demos and Paul were now apparent to all, and your
mother had had it too! There is a little saying still
around TBN that goes like this, "Which would you
rather have: Jan's wrath, or God's wrath?" Most folks
prefer God's wrath, since it holds the promise of much
more mercy!

*"Where were YOU, Demos Shakarian, when God
spoke to Paul Crouch and me simultaneously and called
us to this ministry?"* she shouted! *"Where were YOU
when we were scraping tile and tar off the floor of our
first studio?"* Now her voice was rising and the tears
began to flow. *"Where were YOU, Paul Toberty, when
God moved a mountain for us and brought in $35,000
the day of our deadline for Channel 40? Where were
you BOTH when God gave Paul Crouch the VISION of
satellite and TV stations linked together covering the
land with Christian television?"* she sobbed.

My God, as tough an old German as I am, I was
ready to crawl under a chair somewhere! I think Norm
Juggert was not far behind! I have to confess that this
was the most anointed rebuke I had ever witnessed.
Her "Irish eyes" were not "smiling"—they were
flashing water and fire! Her grandmother Annie Laurie
Greene would have been proud of her!

At the conclusion of that meeting, the conflict was
over—the steam had dissipated—the coup, if it had
been one, had failed. For several minutes you could
have heard a pin drop all over the building. Pale-faced
employees who had heard every word of your mother's

eruption worked feverishly at their desks. We probably got more work done that afternoon, than the rest of the whole week!

Finally, Demos Shakarian spoke. "Jan," he said, "maybe you are right. Perhaps we should all think and pray about the future of TBN."

With that, we adjourned, but it was a NEW DAY for TBN. We had passed an important milestone. Even the atmosphere—the air itself—was different. TBN would go forward.

But the story is far from over, my sons. Remember, I told you this episode has an amazing ending!

CHAPTER 19

"THE BARREN HATH BORN SEVEN"

In spite of every difficulty, in spite of all the dissension and strife, TBN continued to grow. God had given us a powerful word of prophecy during the beginning days of TBN as your mother and Joyce Toberty were interceding in prayer for TBN in the den of our home. By the Holy Spirit, they were directed to the book of Samuel and the prayer of Hannah:

> *Those who were hungry cease*
> *to hunger, so that the barren*
> *gives birth to seven.*
> *I Samuel 2:5 (NASB)*

I was ecstatic at this word since, at this time, the maximum number of full power TV stations permitted by the FCC to one owner was *SEVEN!* I knew in my spirit that we would have these stations, but this was glorious confirmation.

Shortly after this promise was given, we were contacted by a group of businessmen from Phoenix, Arizona. Channel 21 had been purchased by Pastor Lindell Edmonds of Bible Fellowship Church, but was having serious financial problems. Over two million dollars had been raised through the sale of bonds and the church was in default. After many meetings and negotiating sessions, TBN agreed to assume all debts of the station in exchange for the license and assets. This was an awesome responsibility for TBN. It was December of 1975 and we had only been on the air with Channel 40, our first TV station, for a little over a year! I will never forget that historic meeting with about 300, mostly elderly, people who had invested their savings in a Christian TV station that was now unable to pay them back. Your mother and I had been sending "Praise the Lord" and a few other programs over to Phoenix and purchasing some air time so they were basically familiar with TBN, but we were so new—*could we ever pay them back?*

Your mother and I poured out our hearts and vision for a great Christian television network to those precious saints on a Saturday afternoon in Phoenix, Arizona. We promised that we would work till our fingers bled and pray till our knees were calloused to pay them every penny plus interest! Finally, a vote was to be taken, but before ballots could even be passed out, an elderly gentleman stood up and said, "I've heard enough—I believe Paul and Jan will come through—I vote to accept their plan to sell Channel 21 to TBN!" With that, the entire group burst into applause and it was settled. TBN would be endorsed by the bondholders to take control of KPAZ-TV Channel 21 Phoenix, Arizona!

But there were still many hurdles to be crossed. Word spread that TBN had made application to the FCC for the purchase of Channel 21. My sons, believe it or not, it was my Christian brothers that nearly destroyed our whole plan for station number two! This time from two different sources.

Jim Bakker was developing a successful TV ministry back in North Carolina, as we have already discussed. Jim was also pondering the prospect of purchasing whole TV stations for the expansion of his PTL Club and Heritage USA ministry. So he sent his representative to Phoenix and entered into negotiations with Pastor Lindell Edmonds for the purchase of Channel 21. At about the same time, a Christian brother from Seoul, South Korea, entered the picture. He too, through American partners, contacted Pastor Edmonds and entered into negotiations as well.

My sons, even the greatest men of God have feet of clay! All of us who are called of God can miss the perfect will of God at times. I do not cry down from any ivory tower since I, too, have missed the will of God at times, but I tell you of this sad chapter to warn you of the importance of seeking and knowing the PERFECT will of God at each and every point in our lives.

What followed is another dark chapter in this first

expansion of the miracle of TBN. Pastor Edmonds sent a letter cancelling our original agreement to purchase Channel 21 which dashed our hopes and dreams for station number two and the next phase of a great network of stations spanning the continent. For several months it looked as though Channel 21 was finished. Finally the RCA corporation, who owned the main transmission equipment, moved in and repossessed the transmitter. Now the station was off the air!

I will never forget how discouraged and depressed your mother and I had been to receive this news. It seemed, for sure, that all was lost and that Channel 21 would never be ours.

In the midst of this sickening news, "our pastor," Jack Hayford had come to be our special guest on "Praise the Lord." Jack was, and still is, pastor of the historic Church on the Way, in Van Nuys, California.

A few years earlier at a TBN staff meeting, at which Pastor Jack was ministering, the Lord had spoken an important word to me. Kneeling in prayer beside me, I had turned to Pastor Jack and had asked him to be my pastor and as well as a spiritual covering for TBN. He graciously consented and with Anna, his wife, has been a source of wise and godly counsel through the years.

Before the program that night, your mother and I had poured out our hearts to "our pastor." We had explained how unfairly we were being treated. We went into great detail telling how we had already invested over $300,000 in the Phoenix station. That we

had supplied much of the programming—had signed a
legal contract—had filed our FCC application, only to
have the contract broken by the owners. Jack finally
interrupted me in the middle of my tirade and gave me
a word that shocked me! It was a word that I did not
want to hear and at first could not receive. "Paul," he
said gently, "give it up." At first it did not even
register—*give WHAT up?* My pastor went on to
explain. "You and Jan are trying to do this in your own
strength. You have got to give Phoenix up to the Lord.
Tell God that Phoenix is over—a closed chapter in your
life." Well, for an old fighting German, this was not
what I wanted to hear! I was ready to sue for specific
performance—we had a signed contract—it was easily
enforceable in a court of law! After several moments
of rather stunned silence, your mother and I at least
agreed for Jack to lead us in a time of prayer. I will
confess that at this point I did not feel like praying, I
was angry! But, gradually, the presence of the Holy
Spirit began to soften my heart. Your mother began to
weep softly and finally Pastor Jack said, "Paul, will
you follow me in a prayer of release?" Reluctantly I
agreed—it was one of the hardest prayers I have ever
prayed. *"Dear Lord"*—I repeated phrase by phrase—
"I forgive all those who have hurt me." I choked a
little on that one. *"Father, we give Phoenix up to
you...."* Swallowing hard, your mother and I both
repeated, *"...we give Phoenix up...."* A strange new
peace settled upon us—the heavy burden lifted—
Phoenix was now in God's hands. In my mind

Phoenix was gone—forever!

But now, once again, it was God's move! Ah, if ever we could truly learn that the "battle is the Lords!"

Since the equipment had been repossessed, and the station was off the air, the situation was getting desperate. Lawsuits were being filed by bondholders against the owners. The license was even in jeopardy since the FCC will not allow a station to remain off the air indefinitely. TBN partners were so incensed at the developments they brought pressure on the owners, even picketing the station, demanding that the purchase contract with TBN be renewed!

Finally, Pastor Edmonds was back at the table willing to work out a new contract for TBN to assume ownership of Channel 21! After several more difficult negotiating sessions we hammered out a new and much better contract for TBN. By now, the folks at the Phoenix airport were getting to know me—not from being on TV either! Since the financial needs of many of the elderly bondholders was getting desperate, my FCC attorney and I paid a personal visit on all the Arizona senators and congressmen. We asked them to do an unprecedented favor for TBN—would they write a joint letter to the FCC urging speedy consideration of TBN's new contract and application for the license of KPAZ-TV in Phoenix. To our great delight, senators Barry Goldwater, and Dennis De Concini along with all of the Arizona congressmen agreed and signed the very special request to the chairman of the FCC, Mr. Richard Wiley.

The wait was agonizing, as always, but now

because of this special assistance from Congress, we had hope that a decision would come soon. *And soon it was!* In weeks, rather than months, the telegram was flashed: *COMMISSION GRANTED!* The date—July 21, 1977. Arizona and California rejoiced—Channel 21 would be ours—and what a date: *7-21-77!*

Now came the final phase—close of escrow. This is where the property deeds were transferred, attorney fees paid, the new bond payment schedule set up, plus a thousand and one miscellaneous transactions were completed. It was here that Satan made his last stand to stop the transfer—to yet deny TBN station number two.

Because so much time had passed since our original agreement, a number of the bondholders had reached the end of their patience. They, now, demanded payment in full and some of them were board members of the station whose signatures would be required for the closing documents. Others had filed earlier lawsuits and had been awarded judgments by the court. The cries and demands of a few turned into a veritable three-ring circus as they realized that the FCC had approved the license transfer and now this was a real sale!

I must say here that the vast majority of bondholders were precious and generous beyond words! They had agreed to a semi-annual payback with interest over a twelve year period! Some even voluntarily donated some or all of their bonds back to TBN! God bless them! Many have since gone home to Glory—what a reward they have entered into! *Over seven million souls through TBN (that we know of) are credited to their account!*

We finally reached agreement on all but one of the bondholders. I will never forget this final, traumatic meeting in the office of their attorney. $25,000 in cash was demanded or the whole new deal was off! I was angry and incensed that "Christians" would take advantage of this sensitive and critical final stage of our closing, but that was it—their final offer!

I asked for a few minutes to think and pray for direction. This seemed to be literally the straw that would break the camel's back! *"Dear Lord,"* I cried. *"What now?"* The truth was, we did not have the $25,000— besides, even the debt we were assuming looked large and frightening. My faith truly began to waiver.

I called your mother at home in California. I said, "Honey, I don't believe we can handle this. These last bondholders won't budge, they are demanding all cash and we just do not have it." I also explained that under the terms of our agreement these bondholders could actually prevent the closing of escrow and, in effect, the whole deal for Channel 21! Over the phone we began to pray and, as usual, your mother began to cry. As we called out to God for help and direction, she suddenly cried out—at first I wasn't sure if it was a cry of praise or despair! "Honey," she cried! "I just opened my Bible—listen to this!" The scripture was from the prophet Haggai 2:1—

> *In the seventh month, in the one and*
> *twentieth day of the month....*

"The Barren Hath Born Seven"

Dear Lord, regardless of what followed, I immediately recognized that DATE! The FCC had granted the transfer of the license in the *"SEVENTH MONTH"* and on the *"ONE AND TWENTIETH DAY"*—*yes, July 21, 1977!* But there was more—much more!

> *Who is left among you that saw this*
> *house in her first glory? And how do*
> *you see it now? Is it not in your eyes in*
> *comparison of it as nothing?"*

How true! Channel 21 was off the air. It was, indeed, "AS NOTHING"! But here is where it exploded in our spirits:

> *Yet now be strong...saith the Lord...be*
> *strong all ye people of the land, saith the*
> *Lord, and work: for I am with you, saith*
> *the Lord of hosts.*

As the text continued, it was the same as if God Himself was speaking directly to us:

> *I will fill this house with glory saith*
> *the Lord of hosts....*

And here was the clincher—my answer to the financial demands:

> *The silver is mine, and the gold*
> *is mine...the glory of this latter house*
> *shall be greater than the former...*

I Had No Father But God

*and in this place will I give peace,
saith the Lord of hosts.
Haggai 2:1-9*

By now, your mother and I were both weeping and shouting our praises to God! K"PAZ"—means "peace" in Spanish—God's final word was, "In this place will I give peace!" That was it—I had my answer—I went back into the attorney's office and said, "It's a deal, where do I sign?" I knew God would provide the money—CHANNEL 21 was ours, again, only by His miracle. I do not even remember where the money came from, but it was there when we needed it and we *CLOSED THE ESCROW,* changed all the locks on the doors and went crazy putting Channel 21 BACK ON THE AIR. Our engineers worked literally around the clock to reassemble all the equipment that had been repossessed, and in little more than a month KPAZ-TV Channel 21 in Phoenix, Arizona flashed back ON THE AIR with "LET'S JUST PRAISE THE LORD!"

And while in many other places we have had troubles and trials—true to His word, in Phoenix, God has given us *HIS PAZ!*

After all the excitement of Channel 21, the very next year perhaps the most far-reaching and exciting TV station of all was born. Yes, it was in 1978 that the great satellite station came on the air, which I told you about earlier. Soon after, in 1980, we bought Lester Sumrall's full power station in Miami! What a night that was, as we threw the first coast-to-coast switch and linked east and west together—LIVE—for the first time in Christian television history!

One interesting sidelight to our purchase of Channel 45 in Miami was where the down payment came from. As you boys know, we agreed to pay Lester Sumrall TEN MILLION dollars for his station. This is, by the way, the highest price we have ever paid for a TV station. The good news was that he financed half of the purchase price at no interest. But, we still had to have five million dollars at the close of escrow, and we only had half of what we needed, or about two and a half million dollars. Just as we needed the balance, I was approached by HBO. If you have cable TV you know who *Home Box Office* is. They were getting started about the same time our satellite station came on the air. They had a very special need to be on the satellite we were accessing, but it was full—there was no more room. Since we were feeding mostly our own stations, and a few affiliates, it really did not matter that much which satellite we were on. I consulted with Jim Gammon, our FCC attorney, as to how much he thought we could charge them for the switch in satellites. He thought, maybe up to one and a half million dollars. After all, satellite was brand new, no one really knew its value. I said, "Jim, I need two and a half million for Miami!" Jim swallowed hard, but agreed to present the demand. To our great joy and surprise, they accepted without even haggling, giving us the other half of the five million dollars needed for our down payment on Miami! *Miami, you were expensive, but you were worth it!*

One more miracle I have to share while dealing with Miami concerns the huge antenna that sits atop the thousand foot supporting tower.

A short time after we closed the escrow with Lester Sumrall, the antenna and feed-line caught fire and burned out! This was a terrible shock since the repair bill came to about $350,000! So, we had no choice—equipment was ordered and installation begun. Apart from the day God moved a mountain for us, this amazing story I'm about to tell you is probably the greatest physical and visible miracle of all!

The engineers decided the antenna should be lowered into place by a large military style helicopter. Remember, we are dealing with a piece of equipment forty feet long and weighing over two tons! Since this was an extremely hazardous exercise, the trailer park residents living at the base of the thousand foot TV tower had to be evacuated.

The helicopter pilot and engineer were a father and son team—dad few the chopper and the son was positioned atop the TV tower waiting to bolt the huge antenna in place as soon as it was lowered. The cable connecting the antenna to the chopper was designed with a disconnect device which was activated with an explosive charge so that the chopper could break the cable and fly away once the antenna was lowered into place. Father and son were communicating through a pair of two-way radios and all seemed to be going well as the giant helicopter hovered with its precious, but hazardous, burden. We would learn later that the two-way radio system had failed and that father and son had reverted to hand signals for communication.

My sister, Naomi and her husband Bernard Ridings, were managing the station at the time. Your Uncle Bernie gave us the picture from the ground as the four-story tall antenna was lowered a few inches at a time. The pilot's son was waiting, poised to anchor the antenna base to its platform with bolts the size of dinner plates! Frantically, the son was trying to signal his father that he was having trouble getting the bolts to thread properly, but the father interpreted the signal to mean "all is well!" BANG! The explosive charge was triggered and the helicopter flew away with the forty foot tall, two-ton antenna standing on its platform, rocking precariously! Panic stricken, the son worked feverishly for several minutes rotating the large bolts which would finally secure the antenna to its base.

Your Uncle Bernie, who was watching and praying at the bottom of the thousand foot tower, told us that the spirit of the Lord came upon him at this moment and that he began to pray mightily in the Spirit in an unknown tongue! From his vantage point all seemed to be going well, but in his spirit he knew something was wrong!

The story that finally tumbled from an ashen-faced young engineer was a miracle of awesome proportions. With helicopter prop wash blowing full force on the unsecured antenna—*wonder of wonders*, it stood in perfect upright position for several minutes until the final bolt was secured!

Father and son later likened this miracle to standing a long lead pencil on a table with a large fan blowing on it! They actually tried this experiment and could never get the pencil to stand! My sons, I am certain that if we could have looked into the invisible spirit world, we would have seen the hand of God holding that antenna in place.

We asked the young engineer if he knew how to pray and he exclaimed, "I learned how a thousand feet in the air when I heard that umbilical cord blow apart!"

For twelve years, now, that miracle antenna has been beaming 24-hour Christian television up and down the Gold Coast of south Florida. And every time I look up at that giant tower, a special praise to God leaps within my spirit! Yes, God will even override his own laws of physics to protect and keep those who are walking in His perfect will!

Finally, Oklahoma City came on the air in 1981 after a competing applicant finally withdrew. Next, Richmond/Cincinnati came on the air the same year, followed by New York in 1982, and finally, Seattle/Tacoma in 1984. I shall never forget that date for three very special reasons. First of all, as I explained earlier, in 1984 the maximum number of full power stations any one organization could own was seven, and Seattle/Tacoma, Channel 20, was TBN's station number seven.

Secondly, it was March 30, 1984, my 50th birthday, when the news flashed—"KTBW-TV IS ON THE AIR!" Matt, you were there, probably directing

the program, which was a great TBN rally coming from
Hugh Rosenburg's Tri-County Assembly in Cincinnati.
What a night—what a birthday gift! Our joy could
hardly be contained! Seven great full power stations,
and now, affiliated stations were joining us, cable
stations were hooking up, and even our low and
medium power stations were coming on line. And all
linked together LIVE with our great new satellite
station! To cap it all off, one brave partner stood up and
began singing "Happy Birthday"—the whole
congregation joined in—a highlight I will never forget.

But, some very sad news reached us that night—my
third reason for remembering it with very mixed
emotions. In the middle of the live "Praise the Lord"
program the call came—*"Brother Demos Shakarian
has been rushed to the hospital in Los Angeles—a
stroke—please pray!"* We immediately called the
4,000 partners there, plus our TBN family from coast-
to-coast, to intercession and prayer. The nation was
shocked. Demos was one of our great leaders—a
"Father in Israel"—beloved by millions. Oh, how we
prayed! For several days we reported on his progress
and to our great joy, God heard and answered our
prayers. This dairy farmer that God had used to raise
up thousands of Full Gospel Businessmen's chapters
around the world, would live—he would continue to
lead this great fellowship of businessmen to even
greater heights. The Christian world rejoiced.

But the best part of this story, my sons, I tell you now
with even more joy than the joy of our seventh station

signing on the air. Demos had gone through not only some physical deep waters, but also some political ones as well. His stroke had left him in a somewhat weakened condition, but his mind and spirit were perfectly intact—in fact, I have always believed even stronger.

Now, it is one thing to have honest differences of opinion as to the direction and leadership of a ministry or organization, as was the case with Demos and TBN. But it is reprehensible to see ambitious, power-seeking *"Christians"* seek to unseat a God-ordained leader such as Demos Shakarian when he is down physically. But, my sons, that is exactly what happened. A faction of the Full Gospel Businessmen felt that Demos should be "promoted" to "president emeritus" and, in effect, put out to pasture *(how's that for a good dairy term?)*. Your mother and I finally learned of this problem and invited Demos to come and share his burden with the larger Body of Christ, and to support and pray for him and the Full Gospel Businessmen. During this struggle for power *(dear Lord, when will this Body finally grow up?)*, Demos appeared several times and each time he grew stronger both in the Lord as well as in his rightful position as founder and president of Full Gospel Businessmen.

But on this first visit something very special happened that your mother and I will treasure the rest of our lives. And, Matt, as the Lord would have it, you were there to be our witness.

At TBN, there is a long hall leading down to the "Praise the Lord" program set in what we call studio C.

Demos and his aide, who assisted him, had just stepped out of the washroom. Matt, you will recall that you just happened to descend the stairs and ended up a few steps behind Demos. At this point he was totally unaware of your presence. Looking down the hall, Demos spied your mother and me as we turned the corner, heading for the "Praise the Lord" set and the program that evening. We were excited that brother Demos was to be our special guest that night. The hall is not too brightly lit, but finally we could see Demos, who was waving and was trying to get our attention. In hardly more than a hoarse whisper, he began to call out, "Paul and Jan, Paul and Jan!" We quickened our pace and finally met at the door of studio C. For a moment, I feared Demos was ill again as he reached out to grasp our hands. Tears welled up in this great man's eyes as he sobbed, "I'm sorry, I'm so sorry!" We fell into each other's arms and wept our repentance and reconciliation. No explanation was needed— words would have gotten in the way—this was HEALING time—this was God's ordained rendezvous for three wounded souls that God wanted to mend. And mend us He did. Demos continues, at this writing, fully restored to his God-ordained position as leader of the greatest laymen's ministry on earth. Your mother and I have not only found the joy of reconciliation, but a new father in Christ! And, Matt, I am so happy you got to be there and learn!

The final joy to this chapter came even as I was in the final phase of writing this account to you.

Demos Shakarian and Paul Toberty had both resigned from the board of TBN shortly after the traumatic board meeting I described earlier in this chapter. As might be expected, fellowship was broken, and what little relationship remained was strained at best. Gradually, hearts and spirits began to mend as we continued to work with and broadcast some of the great Full Gospel Businessmen's conventions.

Paul Toberty began to acquire Christian radio stations and for a time actually contracted with TBN to use a part of our satellite to distribute the program signal to his radio stations. We were happy to be a small part of God's new direction for Paul and Joyce Toberty who, by the way, own and operate southern California's most successful Christian radio station today.

But the complete healing came in the form of an unexpected letter from Paul just about the time I was writing this chapter. It read in part as follows:

> It has been some time since we left TBN, but I felt that a letter of apology for any mistakes on my part, during our time there, was in order. Yet, I feel the Lord did place us there with you in the beginning, and had the assurance at the time that the ministry would have a great impact in the future. Certainly, this has come to pass.
>
> Trust this is accepted in the spirit in

which it is written, as much as I want
the best for you and your ministry, I, too
want the same.

I was overjoyed to receive this wonderful word
which, in my mind, completed any final healing which
may have been needed. I immediately dictated a return
letter which read in part:

> Dear Paul and Joyce: Thank you from
> both Jan and me for your refreshing and
> healing letter. You both have been
> much on my mind as I am writing the
> 20th anniversary book on the many
> trials and tribulations, but also the many
> joys and victories of TBN.
>
> While Jan and I have long since
> forgiven and to a great deal forgotten the
> trials of the past, we still welcome your
> kind letter with all of our hearts.
>
> We ask that you grant us the same
> forgiveness for anything that we may
> have done to cause hurt or sorrow in any
> of our relationship of the past.

So there you have it, my sons, an important lesson
on broken relationships—some of the causes, but also
the marvelous cure for those who will hear and obey

the command of Christ to FORGIVE.

I wish I could say that all of our problems and heartaches were over, but in a very real sense they were just beginning!   Hold on, this next mountain is a big one!

CHAPTER 20

SADDLEBACK

My sons, we come now to, without a doubt, the most ominous threat ever raised against TBN, and for that matter against all of Christian television. In our entire twenty year history to date, nothing matches *SADDLEBACK!* By now, I have worn out the phrase—"There came yet another valley of testing and despair!" Well, forget it—I won't—no, I can't use that phrase any more because this valley has no equal! Up until now, at least I was at differences with my Christian brothers. As traumatic as all of those encounters were—at least they were my brothers! I never feared for my actual physical life, but Saddleback was DIFFERENT!

But first, a little history so you will understand just how we reached this all time low! Follow carefully, it gets a little complicated.

When we first bought Channel 40, it was licensed to

a little suburb of Los Angeles called Fontana, California. Mr. Lerma, the owner, had received special permission from the FCC to operate his main studio in North Hollywood, which is in the city of Los Angeles. In those days, you were required to locate your main studio in your city of license, unless special permission was granted by the FCC to operate elsewhere. Remember, this all had nothing to do with your transmitter location which was, and still is, Mt. Wilson, next to all the other southern California TV transmitters.

You will remember that TBN had been raised up in the city of Santa Ana which is about fifty miles south of Los Angeles. Fontana is about fifty miles east of Los Angeles, so we wanted neither Fontana nor North Hollywood for our main studio location. We wanted to stay in Santa Ana or at least, in Orange County, which is the large county just south of Los Angeles County.

Since Mr. Lerma had received permission to move his main studio into Los Angeles, we felt the FCC would have no objection to our asking for permission to operate our main studio right where we were in Santa Ana. But when we asked, the FCC said "No, the move will be in accordance with the rules this time. You must go through a 'rule-making' application."

What this meant in simple, laymen's terms was— we would have to move our legal city of license from Fontana to Santa Ana, California. A fairly simple procedure, but there was just one hitch—all the other TV stations in Orange County would have to approve the move. Well, there were only two—the Coast

Community College District station, and Pat Boone's station in Anaheim. The college had no objection, but apparently Pat Boone did! Pat and a group of other Hollywood stars had invested in Channel 56 licensed to Anaheim, just next door to Santa Ana. Pat, along with Jimmy Durante, Fess Parker, and several other celebrities were developing Orange County's first commercial TV station. At first, I could not understand their objections—why would Pat or his partners care if Channel 40 moved its city of license to Santa Ana? After all, we were already there operating under a temporary permit until the matter was resolved. I also pointed out that TBN was, and always would be, 100% Christian—certainly no threat to the commercial operations of Channel 56! Pat presented this to his business partners, but they objected, "What if TBN would ever sell Channel 40?" A new buyer could conceivably operate it as a commercial station and Pat's partners feared the competition. I pleaded with Pat, but since he was not in a majority control position, even though he was president, my pleas were denied.

Since Pat's partners were not in agreement, this opened up a very narrow and very curious rule of FCC law. Again, in simple laymen's terms, it meant we could file for the move to Santa Ana, but it also meant that ANYONE ELSE could also file for the new Santa Ana license *of OUR Channel 40!* This sounded ominous, indeed, but the alternative was to either move all of TBN out to Fontana, or up to Los Angeles. Finally, after much thought and consultation, we

173

decided to take the chance and file for the move to Santa Ana—*a big mistake!* Mr. Gammon had warned us that we could draw a competing application, but that our chances were good, since TBN was the incumbent licensee, and we were actually on the air. What Jim Gammon did not know was something I would have to learn over the next five years and at the cost of one million dollars in legal fees. Follow this closely, if you've got the stomach for it, because before we are through with this chapter, it may cause you to feel as much pain as I still do over this nightmare now past.

It seems there is a class of unscrupulous lawyers out there who read carefully each day the record of the FCC. When they see an application filed, they encourage a friend, or a friend of a friend, to file a competing application against it. The lawyer knows that win, lose, or draw, he gets his fee. And his client most always gets bought out by the incumbent, so he and his client all go home richer! It's a dirty business. Fortunately the rules of the FCC have been changed to prevent most of this trafficking in TV licenses today.

I hope I'm not boring you boys, but I have to lay a foundation for the absolutely unique conditions which triggered this new nightmare that was about to break upon TBN. What makes this all the more maddening, in retrospect, is the fact that new rules of the FCC now permit you to place your main studio anywhere you want under your main city grade coverage, so today we would not even have to seek FCC approval. God bless President Reagan for many of these kinds of changes and relief from government red tape!

So, we filed for the move and waited the mandatory thirty days, holding our breath to see if anyone else would file for our Channel 40 license. I know you remember along with me—*THEY DID!*

It is interesting to note and remember the timing of this competing application for the license of Channel 40. In April of 1978, we had just broken through and signed our new satellite station on the air. Surely all the hosts of hell were aroused, because in less than thirty days, the very next month in May of 1978, a competing application was filed against the license of Channel 40, seeking to take it away from us for commercial purposes.

Naturally, the first thing you want to know when your TV license is filed against is: *WHO is the competitor?* We investigated and learned to our dismay that these were serious competitors made up of a group of very wealthy Orange County businessmen. One of the partners was Mr. John Virtue, who was also the president of Saddleback Broadcasting Company, our competitor. Mr. Malcomb Klein, was his manager and point man, along with all the right ingredients to make for a serious threat to our Channel 40 license. *Merciful God, now what!*

TBN was beginning to expand, but Channel 40 and southern California was still 95% of our support. If Channel 40 fell, that would have been the end of TBN. A panic seized my soul that I had never felt before—a sickness in the pit of my stomach that would not leave me day nor night for the next five, long, agonizing years!

Now the battle began in earnest. The best way to take someone's TV license away from them is to find something wrong with their operations. So, our competitors visited us day after day—inspecting our public file—taping everything we broadcast—hovering, searching, spying on everything we did.

Your mother and I soon realized that we were being personally spied upon by a private detective. He followed us most everywhere we went. We actually got to know him and would wave once in a while as we left our home. Our attorneys advised us that this was fairly routine—if they could catch your mother or me in some unethical or illegal activity, this would be a point against TBN, and a point in their favor as we approached the trial or hearing date to see who would receive the license of Channel 40.

Finally, the other shoe fell—our competitors, in carefully examining our latest license application, found to our dismay, an inaccurate and, in fact, untruthful statement in it! I had assigned the license applications to our program director, Mr. Jim Lynn, who had supervised the many functions, forms, and legwork involved in filing for our license renewals. The one foot thick application was then forwarded to our FCC attorney for filing with the Commission. The inaccurate statement had to do with certain dates that interviews had been conducted with community leaders, which was one of the requirements for the license application. Someone had handwritten a date of when these interviews had been conducted, which upon careful investigation by our competitors, turned out to be false. The FCC is usually very understanding, and even merciful as concerns ignorant and unintentional mistakes, but if you *EVER* lie or misrepresent anything to the FCC—look out, you will almost always be disqualified, and your license will be forfeited! Fortunately, the inaccurate statement had been, as I said, handwritten, so everyone at TBN, including myself, had to submit to a handwriting analysis expert to determine who had misrepresented the information. Oh, what agony, and the stakes were so very high. The license and the very survival of TBN was at stake.

In the meantime, depositions were ordered. Your mother and I, along with many of the staff, and some of our programmers, were subpoenaed to testify under oath about the various programming, engineering, and finances of TBN. It was wicked and gruelling. Worst of all, we had a gag order and we could not even ask our partners to pray for us since any mention of this battle could give TBN an unfair advantage over our competitors under FCC rules. The darkness and despair settled in upon my soul so heavily that at times I couldn't even pray. A *Gone with the Wind* sized novel could be written about this ordeal that seemed would never end, but time nor space would permit that, nor would it serve any useful purpose.

Finally, in total despair, I fell upon my office floor and told God—"Either you release me from this horror, or take me home!" I flung my Bible open, half in desperation and half in anger! My eyes fell on Jeremiah 40! Just above that very special number, these words leaped off the page at me:

> *But I will deliver thee in that day,*
> *saith the Lord: and thou shalt not*
> *be given into the hand of the men*
> *of whom thou art afraid.*
>
> *For I will surely deliver thee...*
> *because thou hast put thy trust*
> *in me, saith the Lord.*
> *Jeremiah 39:17, 18*

If God, Himself, had stepped through the wall and spoken to me in person, He could not have said anything more comforting or more encouraging at that moment. I was in absolute awe of the word God had given me at my lowest point, physically, mentally, and spiritually. With that promise and assurance, I arose to face another day and another battle.

Finally, our break came! In February of 1981, it was our turn to depose all of the Saddleback principals and employees. As a result, the administrative law judge granted three serious qualifying issues against Saddleback! It seems they had not crossed every "T" nor dotted every "I" either in their application.

Our attorney had taken some Saddleback depositions on a Friday, and I had hoped to hear how they went, but Jim Gammon never called that day. Your mother and I retired that night as usual, grateful for the weekend that promised a little respite from our storm. I could not have imagined the spiritual encounter I was to have early the next morning.

I'm not sure if I have ever recounted this experience with you, but this was, perhaps, the most unusual and exhilarating spiritual experience I have ever had. It must have been about daybreak, because a faint light was just beginning to show under the thick blackout drapes. Your mother was still asleep at my side when suddenly it felt as if I was actually rising up from my bed—*seeming to float as if lifted by the hand of God!* For a moment, I thought I must be dreaming—but no—there was your mother, there were the curtains—all the furniture, and familiar surroundings were in place. Suddenly, I heard the voice of the Lord more clearly and distinctly than I ever had before—His word virtually echoed in my spirit:

THE YOKE OF THE OPPRESSOR
IS BROKEN!
THE YOKE OF THE OPPRESSOR
IS BROKEN!

This sentence was repeated several times as I began to feel an absolute state of euphoria! It was glorious—I was floating ever higher. *"Dear Lord, am I being translated?"*

Slowly I returned to normal as this most wonderful and exhilarating encounter faded. *"What could it mean?"*

I wondered. *"When would I know what it meant?"* For some time—I can't even imagine how long, I simply lay there in the afterglow of this experience. Surely it had something to do with the Saddleback ordeal, *but what?* When your mother awoke, I told her of this unusual encounter and together we prayed for God to reveal the meaning.

I didn't have long to wait!

Early Monday morning, Jim Gammon called. He was ecstatic. "Paul, I deposed their engineer last Friday, they don't even have a transmitter site, plus there are a lot of other things in their engineering that I think completely disqualifies them. I'll keep on checking and will be in touch!" In just a few days, a call came from Saddleback's attorney—the first hint that his client would like to enter into a "settlement conference." Translation: "Pay our expenses so far and we will dismiss our competing application." Over the next several months many phone calls were exchanged, settlement offers proposed, and mountains of memos and letters exchanged. By fall we had made a deal, and on October 6, 1981, in Mr. John Virtue's office, we signed the agreement for Saddleback to DISMISS their competing application for TBN's Channel 40! We rejoiced, but the battle was far from over. The matter of our inaccurate application and the mysterious handwriting was still an unresolved issue. The FCC designated our renewal for a hearing before an administrative law judge at the FCC—our Channel 40 license was not yet a sure thing.

We paid our competitor's costs, plus many thousands of dollars to our own attorneys; not to mention the new grey hair that had grown more apparent, nor the horrible knot in the pit my stomach, which had lasted nearly five long years.

In the next chapter, my sons, I will give you the final thrill ride as we exit the Saddleback encounter forever. And, I'll throw in the Merv Mattlock episode for good measure! Are you still sure you want to follow old dad's footsteps into Christian TV? We'll see, won't we—the ride is far from over!

CHAPTER 21

SADDLEBACK II

In the midst of the final throes of the Saddleback affair, your mother and I were to receive another *below-the-belt punch* that was, perhaps, the most outrageous blow of all!

I had invited Aquilla Wilkins Nash, a dear sister and pastor from Longview, Texas, to minister to our staff at TBN and to be a guest on "Praise the Lord." Aquilla is also, without doubt, an anointed prophetess of the Lord, and has spoken many things to your mother and me in the Spirit. I can testify that every word she has ever given to TBN, or to your mother and me personally, has come to pass *exactly* as prophesied. Our prayer meeting had ended and Aquilla, your mother, and I were walking toward my office when we passed one of our staff members in the hall. Suddenly, Aquilla stopped abruptly and said, "Who was that man?" "Oh, that's Merv Mattlock, our 'Praise the

Lord' announcer," your mother replied. After a long, thoughtful pause, Aquilla said, "That man is a snake in your midst, and will cause you great harm! Watch out for him!" Your mother and I were shocked! *Merv, a threat to TBN?* Why, Merv had always been the most gentle, the most kind, and even the most quiet, young man we had on staff. I must confess that I simply did not receive Aquilla's word that day—I actually thought, "She's missed it this time," and really did not give the matter much more thought. Besides, I was too busy preparing for the final hearing on our Channel 40 license at the FCC. We were forced to conduct a full-blown investigation as to who, and how, that incorrect statement got incorporated into our license application. Let me quickly say that while I did not make the mistake, nor did I personally misrepresent anything to the Commission, I had signed the final page of the application, thereby certifying that to the best of my knowledge and belief, everything in it was true and correct. My mistake was quite simply that I had *not* read every page of the application which, as I said before, was over *ONE FOOT thick!* I had delegated that task to Jim Lynn, and other staff members, as well as to our FCC lawyers. Another BIG mistake!

With this gigantic task, along with all my regular duties—hosting "Praise the Lord," writing the monthly newsletter, and a thousand and one other things—I was *not* prepared for the knock on my office door, nor the visit I was about to receive.

Standing before me was Merv Mattlock—not too

unusual, although visits such as this were fairly rare. I assumed that there must be some question about the "Praise the Lord" guest line-up for that evening. But it did not take long for me to realize that this was no ordinary visit! Merv was trembling and very obviously agitated in both spirit and body. For a rather long and awkward moment he just stood there saying nothing. Finally, sensing that we had a real problem here, I beckoned him to be seated over on the couch. Finally, with quavering voice, Merv spoke. "Paul," he said, "I am here today representing a number of spiritual leaders. I have the unpleasant task...," his voice was now breaking with frequent throat clearing and coughing. "My task is to demand your immediate resignation as president of TBN." At this point I did not know whether to be amused or angry. Surely this was some kind of a sick joke! But as Merv continued, I began to realize—*this was NO JOKE!* He continued, "We have evidence that Jan is morally unfit to serve TBN, and that you have mismanaged the financial and business affairs of TBN. I have been commissioned to take charge of TBN to restore order and integrity to this ministry!" With that he handed me a letter demanding my resignation signed by himself alone. An 8.5 richter scale earthquake could not have rocked me more violently! You have heard the old saying, "He was so mad he could see RED?" Let me tell you that it is not just a poetic saying—**I LITERALLY SAW RED!** I arose angrily and moved toward Merv who, recognizing his folly, was now retreating rapidly through the back door of my office. Your mother, hearing the commotion from the room next door, bumped headlong into Merv with me in hot pursuit! Thank God for your mother that day! She succeeded in restraining my fury and persuaded us to sit down and see what in heaven's name was happening. Merv was now violently shaking as he nervously eyed me.

The details of the accusations I will not even dignify by mentioning. Every one of them was proved to be absolutely false as we submitted them to our board and elders. "So, who are these *SPIRITUAL LEADERS* that you represent?" your mother asked. Merv would identify only one—*John Wesley Fletcher*—who was back at Heritage USA in Charlotte, North Carolina. I immediately picked up the phone and got right through to John. When confronted by the allegations, and his participation in Merv Mattlock's *coup d'etat,* he categorically denied any knowledge of, or participation in, Merv's insane demands. Finally, after Merv refused to name any of the *other* "spiritual leaders" who had commissioned him to confront me, I turned to Merv once more, telling him that he had ten minutes to clean out his desk and remove himself from the premises of TBN!

To this day, I am not sure just what, or who, prompted this unspeakable attack on your mother and me—I will never believe that Merv was acting solely on his own. And now, we will probably never know because, well, there is yet one amusing and one tragic episode to the Merv Mattlock affair. We'll deal with that in a succeeding chapter.

By now, we were nearing the trial date of our FCC hearing. Remember, boys, the license of Channel 40 was still on the line. The false statement, in simple terms, certified that certain community leadership interviews had been conducted in a certain month, when indeed, they had not been. The burning question was, *"whose mysterious handwriting was it on the application?"* Jim Lynn, who had supervised the application, steadfastly denied it was his! The two secretaries who assisted Jim also denied any culpability. *So who?* Also, to mystify the whole matter even more, this page in question had been cut mysteriously and a new portion scotch-taped over the original section! Oh, how I wished I had read and wept over each and every page! *"Could some enemy have doctored our application?"* I wondered. The handwriting expert finally issued his findings—the handwriting, he believed, was Jim Lynn's; but Jim still declared, under oath, that he had no recollection, whatsoever, of writing this false statement on our application. Ultimately, it was my time to take the witness stand. I was sworn in and the questioning began. The FCC prosecutors were merciless—*"Did you realize that by signing the application you were certifying that everything in it was true and correct?"* "Yes," was my unqualified answer. *"Didn't you realize that it was your responsibility to assure yourself that every page was, indeed, true and correct?"* My response was, "I thought I had, by assigning the task to my senior staff members, as well as to our FCC attorneys." Finally, the question that I knew would ultimately come—*"Did you, Paul F. Crouch, KNOW that this incorrect and untrue statement was contained in the application at the time you signed it?"*

Throughout all of the hearing and testimony I held my small Bible in my hand, or had it within reach at all times. Ignoring the attorneys, who had mercilessly grilled me all afternoon, I turned to the judge on his bench and said, "Your honor, I respect the authority of this court, and the pursuit of truth and justice for which it stands. But, your honor," I continued, "I also answer to a higher court and Judge who is the Author of this Book I hold in my hand." With that, I laid my Bible out on the table at my side and placed my hand squarely upon it. "Your honor," I concluded, "I swear by Almighty God that I did not know there was a false and inaccurate statement in the application in question." The judge and I maintained total eye contact as I answered the final question as truthfully as I knew how before God and man. I could see it immediately in the judge's eyes—*he believed me*—I knew this nightmare was nearing an end!

Even so, the wheels of justice move exceedingly slow at the FCC. The original hearing order had been issued in October of 1980. We had signed our release with Saddleback in October of 1981. I had given testimony in July of 1982, but the final decision of Judge Thomas B. Fitzpatrick was not released until January 17, 1983.

SADDLEBACK II

In his "Ultimate Findings Of Fact And Conclusion Of Law," Judge Fitzpatrick wrote, among many other things, the following:

> It is concluded that TBN is not disqualified to be a licensee and that the public interest would be served by a grant of its application.

In another paragraph the judge continued:

> The record establishes that Crouch was unaware when he signed the application that it contained a misrepresentation.... As a consequence, Crouch is innocent of any misrepresentation or wrongdoing.

And, finally, the most blessed line of all in conclusion:

> Accordingly, it is ordered, that...the construction permit application of TBN, Inc. is GRANTED.

The decision was released to the public record on January 25, 1983 and became final fifty days later on March 16, 1983! The nightmare had ended—the morning had come! We were free to remain in Orange County, with a waiver to keep our main studios in the suburb of Tustin, California, right next door to Santa

Ana, California, our NEW city of license.

But, my sons, there is a most interesting and blessed postscript to the whole Saddleback affair. You will remember that John Virtue, a prominent Orange County attorney, had been the president of this group that had tried desperately to take the license of Channel 40 from us. It was at least three or four years after the conclusion of the Saddleback chapter that I received a personal call from none other than John Virtue.

"Paul," he said, "I just wanted to call and tell you that your guest on 'Praise the Lord' last night really got to me!" For a moment I had to think—*ah yes*—another lawyer, Gene Neill, the Miami "lawyer criminal" who had been sentenced to fifty years in federal prison. Mr. Virtue continued, "I also want to say how personally sorry I am for all of the pain we surely caused you." I assured John of our unconditional forgiveness, that as believers in Jesus Christ, we were commanded to forgive, and that I hoped he had found his peace with God. He assured me that he had, and in conclusion, asked me to convey his thanks and best wishes to his fellow lawyer, Gene Neill, who had been saved in federal prison, and then released from his fifty year sentence by a miracle of God. We concluded in wishing each other well as we continued our mutual lives and futures.

My sons, remember this truth and scripture well, for it is an important key to your future blessings and success:

Saddleback II

When a man's ways please the Lord,
he will cause even his enemies to be
at peace with him.
Proverbs 16:7

We move, now, to the final battle in this first twenty year odyssey of TBN.

CHAPTER 22

JOSEPH'S BRETHREN — THE NRB

After the Saddleback ordeal, I hoped, I prayed, that God would give us a respite from the ceaseless and merciless attacks that had besieged us, it seemed, from the first day that God had spoken to your mother and me, and called us to this incredible theater of spiritual warfare. Actually, God did, and for the next several years, TBN entered into the most awesome period of spiritual and numerical growth we had ever experienced.

In 1983, President Reagan declared, "THE YEAR OF THE BIBLE" and we joined, joyfully, with Dr. Bill Bright and many other evangelical leaders in highlighting the word of God and calling for its renewal at home, in our churches, and in our institutions of higher learning. The A.C.L.U. filed suit, but before the courts could even consider the matter, 1983 had ended. We had celebrated "THE YEAR OF

THE BIBLE" and our opposition's objections were moot and outdated.

The next few years were years of unprecedented growth and victories. As I have commented so often, the first decade of TBN produced three TV stations, while the second decade produced over *300* TV stations! Looking back, I can see clearly why Satan tried desperately to destroy us in the early stages—he knew we were on the threshold of the most explosive growth in the history of the Christian church. He knew that *GOD'S NETWORK* was poised to invade his cherished strongholds: *THE AIRWAVES!* As I have reminded the evil one so often—he is only *TEMPORARILY* the "prince of the power of the air." He must and WILL yield his dominion of the airwaves, as *GOD'S TV NETWORK* pierces his traditional domain!

For the next several years, TV stations flashed ON THE AIR in unprecedented numbers. Affiliate stations joined the TBN network; low power and full power stations signed on the air at an average of one a week! Cable stations joined so fast, we could not even count them!

Our one *"HOLY BEAMER"* mobile satellite truck, which TBN pioneered in the late 1970's, now became four "holy beamers" criss-crossing the nation, bringing the great spiritual events of the Body of Christ— *LIVE*—into millions of homes across America.

Then, *wonder of wonders,* foreign nations began opening up to Christian TV! Our first station on foreign soil was Nevis-St. Christopher in the eastern Caribbean Islands, followed by stations in El Salvador,

Belize, Guatemala, Italy, and South Africa. Chinese "Praise the Lord," Haitian "Praise the Lord," and Indonesian "Praise the Lord" swelled the airwaves with the glory of the Lord! It seemed we were *finally free*—on our way to preach *"THIS GOSPEL"* to every creature!

But in 1987—*Wham! It hit!* First the PTL scandal, followed by the Jimmy Swaggart revelations, and to a lesser degree, many others were also drawn into the "TV EVANGELIST" era. TBN was able to remain largely above the fray, but the fallout was universal. Every Christian ministry in the nation was affected to some degree. For months, even years, the failures of a few dominated the secular, and even the religious, news. It seemed that every institution in the land followed suit, with the savings and loans scandals; the stock market scandals—even the Congressional banking scandals. The secular media, and especially the tabloid papers, had their "scandal heyday" as obscure names all the way to world famous names, met their day of reckoning, had their day in court, and some went to prison for varying crimes and terms. Events of the late 1980's brought to mind the warning of the Apostle Paul, who wrote:

> *Yet once more I shake not only the earth,*
> *but also heaven...so that*
> *those things which cannot*
> *be shaken may remain.*
> *Hebrews 12:26, 27*

TBN had already been "shaken" so many times we had lost count, but there was to be, yet another shaking!

This time it was directed at me, personally, and broke in January of 1988, as I registered for the National Religious Broadcasters' convention in Washington, D.C. I had been a member and a supporter of NRB for many years, attending and participating in its many worthwhile and interesting activities. For one thing, the Commissioners of the FCC always spoke to us, giving us the latest in rules and regulations, which was invaluable to broadcasters. Most years the President of the United States came and addressed the members, offering encouragement and admonition, to us in the religious broadcasting field. It was also a time of fellowship and learning, as we attended and participated in the many workshops and conferences, culminating always in a great awards banquet, where various broadcasters and station owners were honored for years of service and special achievements. I was especially excited because TBN was to be honored this year as the outstanding foreign broadcaster of the year in recognition of the new foreign stations coming on line. But, as I registered, several friends and acquaintances came to me privately and said, "Paul, we hear that Paul Roper is calling a news conference tomorrow to charge you with moral failures. We understand that two women will testify of various affairs with YOU!" I was stunned and sickened by what I knew was a lie of the lowest sort. But, Paul Roper had gained national notoriety in the

Jim Bakker scandal, and just the mention of his name seemed to add credibility to the rumor. The morning came with no press conference or announcement as predicted. I called Mr. Colby May, our FCC attorney, and asked him to confer with me. I also called Mr. Philip Little, a private investigator, who had helped us with numerous other difficulties, and asked him to fly to Washington immediately for consultation. The next day I was summoned to the room of Dr. Thomas Zimmerman, one of the executive board members of NRB. Dr. Zimmerman was also the General Superintendent of the Assemblies of God, and had been my pastor in Springfield, Missouri, during most of my growing up years. He had also baptized me in water as I gave my public confession of faith at twelve years of age.

The news he gave me was ominous. "Paul," he said, "the brethren have heard that moral allegations are going to be brought against you, and we have decided that the award that was to be presented to you tonight should be withheld until this matter is cleared up." Now, I was incensed! "Brother Zimmerman," I said, "this rumor has not a shred of truth to it and I demand a meeting with the *"BRETHREN"* who have made this decision without so much as one word of inquiry to me!" Brother Zimmerman was sympathetic and agreed to call a meeting of the full board of the NRB the next afternoon. Within hours, I had my meeting, flanked by my FCC attorney, and my private investigator. I demanded to hear their evidence, or to meet my accusers. To my dismay, the decision to withhold the TBN award that night was based on pure rumor and hearsay! Not one witness—not one fact could be presented. Finally, after much discussion, I reached for my Bible, and laying my hand upon it, said, "Gentlemen, I swear by Almighty God, at the peril of my eternal soul burning in Hell, that I have never touched a woman other than my wife, in a sexual way, either before or after marriage!" For several moments the board members sat in stunned silence. Finally, Dr. Robert Cook, president of NRB, spoke. "Paul, we owe you an apology. Will you stay and let us honor you with the broadcaster award as planned?" When he saw I was struggling with the decision, he continued. "Let us apologize to you BIG, tonight!"

Frankly, I was ready to shake the dust off my feet on the NRB; in fact, I had already called my pilot and ordered him to warm up the engines on Eagle I! But, Bob Cook, great statesman that he was, won the day. That night, I sat at a place of honor next to my former pastor, Dr. Thomas Zimmerman, and TBN was honored as scheduled with the Foreign Broadcaster of the Year award.

The rumors were laid to rest, and since Paul Roper vehemently denied any knowledge or complicity with this attack, it remains a mystery to this day as to who originated this reprehensible lie.

So now my honor was restored, my good name reinstated in the membership roll of the NRB, *right?* Guess again, my sons. Round two is coming up. It's

about to get really nasty this time!   Want to hear more?
Read on.

CHAPTER 23

TO NRB, OR NOT TO NRB

You would think by now that your mother and I should have developed hides as thick as rhinoceros', but as I told you earlier, when the wounds come from your *"brothers"* in Christ—the pain is indescribable!

But before going any further, let's put all modern day Christian suffering into proper perspective. Compared to what Jesus suffered for us—well, none of us have *really* suffered very much, have we? Also, compared to many of the early disciples and followers of Christ, we have also suffered very little. Read <u>Fox's Book of Martyrs</u> and we must all hang our heads in shame for ever complaining about any suffering or hardship for following Jesus.

In some ways, however, the assassination of your good name and character can be just as—if not more—painful than a physical execution. At least if they kill you physically you are instantly with Christ! On the other hand, vicious, lying rumors and attacks aimed at the very heart of your character protract the pain and suffering over many months and even years.

Such was the case with this second wave assault— this time from the *"Ethics Committee"* of the National Religious Broadcasters.

It all started in late January of 1989. Jan and I had missed the NRB convention that year, having scheduled a series of TBN live "Praise the Lord" programs beginning in Phoenix, Arizona. We were "having church" at Pastor Don Price's great Valley Cathedral. A great breakthrough had come and well over 1,000 phoned in one night to receive Christ—it was glorious! Remember in my introduction I spoke of a night that I threw a thousand salvation slips into the air in ecstasy as partners rejoiced from coast-to-coast? Well, this was the time of that great spiritual revival. I suppose we should have braced ourselves—it always seems that an all out satanic attack comes on the heels of great spiritual breakthroughs. On the other hand, these dark valleys and spiritual assaults from the evil one usually signals a great spiritual or physical VICTORY up ahead as well!

My sons, beware if there are no spiritual battles in your lives and ministries. As much as we do dread them, they are most always the proof that we are accomplishing something for God—that we are damaging the kingdom of darkness. If you don't "mess" with the devil, he usually won't "mess" with you! Well, by 1989 we had just passed the 100 TV station mark, so we were *messing* with the devil for sure!

Well, the second NRB bombshell landed January 31, 1989 with a call from Mark Pinsky, a reporter for *The Los Angeles Times*. He stated to my secretary, Margie Tuccillo, that he had a copy of a complaint that had been filed with the NRB Ethics Committee against TBN and Paul Crouch. When Margie asked for details about this "complaint" he refused any further comment, demanding to speak only to Paul Crouch. He did say that his deadline was Wednesday and that a major article would break in the February 2 issue of *The Times.*

And BREAK it did! Without warning or any contact whatsoever from the NRB, the Thursday morning February 2, 1989 issue of the *L.A. Times* read: "ETHICS PANEL INVESTIGATING CROUCH, TBN." We learned later that the same story broke in several other papers across the States, primarily in cities where TBN had major TV stations. The article began as follows:

> Paul F. Crouch, founder and president of Tustin-based Trinity Broadcasting Network, is under investigation by the ethics committee of the National Religious Broadcasters, committee chairman Richard Bott Sr. has confirmed.

The Times article continued:

> Bott, who was interviewed before the
> NRB convention, declined to provide
> details. But according to a 17-page
> complaint submitted to the ethics
> committee—copies of which have been
> given to *The Times*...."

Of course, Mr. Bott did not need to provide details of
the charges—*The Times* reporter had been furnished with
a complete copy of the complaint! Naturally, Mr. Pinsky
refused to reveal his "UNNAMED SOURCES," and it
remains a mystery to this day as to just *who* gave a copy
of this complaint to *The Times*, but here is the *ZINGER!*

The L.A. Times article appeared, as I said, on
February 2. The letter from Mr. Bott of the NRB
which gave TBN its first glimpse of the charges was
dated *FEBRUARY 8!*

The Times article continued:

> The complaint against Crouch was filed
> by the Rev. Heath Kaiser of Dallas. In
> a telephone interview...Kaiser said he
> has been battling Crouch in the courts
> and before the Federal Communications
> Commission for...control of WTBY-TV
> Channel 54, in Poughkeepsie, New
> York.

It is interesting to note that later in the same article
Kaiser, himself, admitted that:

TO NRB, OR NOT TO NRB

> There is no action pending before the
> FCC which has granted a license for
> Channel 54 to Trinity without
> reservation.

When the documents relating to the purchase of the
New York station were examined, and the truth
revealed, it became abundantly clear that TBN had
purchased Channel 54 from Mr. Kaiser and his several
partners in complete compliance with all of the terms
and conditions of the agreement. Trinity not only paid
the full contract price in excess of three million dollars
for a TV station that was totally insolvent and on the
verge of bankruptcy, but as a gesture of goodwill and
compassion, after the contract was signed, we agreed
voluntarily to add an extra sixteen percent above and
beyond the agreed purchase price of the stock. We
provided this additional consideration to aid each
shareholder, including Mr. Kaiser, for extra legal and
accounting expenses they had incurred. We felt this
was a generous act on our part, but our reward was to
become embroiled in a complicated and protracted
lawsuit which lasted over seven years.

Not only had Mr. Kaiser participated in this lawsuit
against TBN, but had also assisted and encouraged
other former employees of Channel 54 to file
complaints with the FCC, culminating in Mr. Kaiser's
own petition to the FCC seeking the denial of our
scheduled license renewal. This prompted a full-scale
field investigation by the staff of the FCC which

resulted in WTBY-TV Channel 54's unconditional renewal of its station license. The FCC found Mr. Kaiser's charges and complaints to be totally without merit! Even after the FCC had ruled in our favor, Mr. Kaiser still filed these same charges with the NRB which he knew had been dismissed by the FCC!

Additional charges in the NRB complaint included the fact that TBN had built new Christian TV stations in areas or near areas where existing Christian TV stations were operating. This was true, but my response was, and is, that *ALL TV stations ought to be CHRISTIAN!* Other Christian operators have built second and even third Christian stations in cities where TBN has stations without any protest on our part. *I praise God for every one!* There is hardly a market in the nation that does not have one or more Christian radio stations—why should there be a limit on TV stations? Each station and operator brings a unique and needed emphasis to the viewer, so I still declare—*build MORE Christian TV and radio stations!* If we are all moving in the will of God, HE will bless and provide for all!

Another charge was an outright misrepresentation! It was alleged that when TBN purchased Channel 21 in Phoenix, Arizona, as I explained earlier, we had assumed over two million dollars in bond indebtedness that was in default. We had assumed this debt, but the misrepresentation alleged that TBN had defaulted by offering the bondholders a tax deductible receipt in lieu of the cash they were entitled to! The record here was and is clear—except for a few who had voluntarily donated their bonds, TBN, through its sister corporation, Trinity of Arizona, PAID EACH AND EVERY BONDHOLDER IN FULL, *two years ahead* of the agreed upon schedule of redemption!

I could write another book on the other baseless charges which I will not even dignify by detailing here. I could add more chapters telling of Mr. Kaiser's other attempts to stop our addition of new TV stations in Seattle, Canton-Akron, and even our initial efforts in South Africa. It seemed for a time that every application we filed at the FCC was met by some objection or petition to deny filed by Mr. Kaiser! All of Mr. Kaiser's filings were overruled or found to be meritless by the FCC, but of course, these actions needlessly drained resources and energies from TBN and the Kingdom of God.

We learned later that *SOMEONE* had also distributed copies of this seventeen page confidential complaint throughout the entire constituency of the NRB! When we requested a copy of the procedures that the NRB Ethics Committee would be following in this investigation, we received no reply! We realized, finally, that we were being thrust into a form of litigation without even knowing what the ground rules were!

Finally, eight days after the news of these charges were plastered all over the front pages of newspapers from coast-to-coast, we received our letter from Mr. Richard Bott, chairman of the Ethics Committee of the NRB. Enclosed was the seventeen page complaint signed, under oath, by Heath Kaiser. We were given thirty days to respond to the charges.

I immediately responded with a letter to Mr. Bott demanding a face-to-face meeting with my accuser at which I agreed to provide complete documentation as to the falsity and absurdity of the allegations. My request was never even responded to! I also instructed Mr. Colby May, our FCC counsel, to contact the legal counsel for the NRB, Mr. Lawrence W. Secrest III, in Washington, D.C. Since the Ethics Committee was supposed to be acting as an impartial arbitrator in this matter, we were appalled by Mr. Bott's actions. In Mr. May's letter to NRB counsel he stated in part:

> I am enclosing copies of articles from the Los Angeles Times, the Poughkeepsie Journal and today's Orange County Register. As you will see, Dick Bott is quoted extensively on the matter, and I am sure you will agree his remarks violate the NRB's own code of conduct and confidentiality for such items.

For days my attorneys and I prepared our eleven page detailed response proving with voluminous documentation and exhibits the falsity of each charge. Stacks of sworn affidavits, reams of official records from the files of the FCC, decisions of other governmental agencies and courts of law were assembled for presentation. By the time we had finished our work the letter and exhibits were several inches thick!

But before we could complete our work on the first attack, the second bombshell landed! Mr. Bott's second letter enclosed another list of complaints, this time from our old nemesis, Merv Mattlock. It was basically a rehash of his earlier financial and moral charges when he had marched into my office demanding my resignation as president of TBN. Naturally, this second charge made its rounds through the news media with new stories of gruesome details of how cruel your mother and I were to all our employees! Every single charge was either an outright lie or a half truth that led to an absolutely false conclusion. Again, I will not dignify these accusations by responding to them, nor waste good time and paper reciting his totally unsubstantiated rumors, but a little comic relief is needed about here!

When Merv had left us rather abruptly, after his unfounded accusations, he moved to Tulsa, Oklahoma to work with Kenneth Hagin Ministries. The word had circulated back through the TBN staff that Merv was now *"in charge"* of all Hagin TV and radio ministries, a much better and more responsible job than he previously held as "Praise the Lord" announcer at TBN. We were happy that he had found a new job which he seemed to be doing well in.

But I will never forget the night that "Dad" Hagin had driven over from Tulsa to Oklahoma City to be our special guest on "Praise the Lord." I did not know it until after the program that Merv had driven Dad, along with his son Ken Hagin, Jr., to the studio that night. Shortly before the program was to begin I walked into the men's rest room only to behold a sight that shall forever be etched into the recesses of my memory. It is one I shall also cherish as long as I live.

There at the wash basin stood Dr. Kenneth Hagin in his stocking feet with red Oklahoma mud caked up to his knees! There on the pullman sat his beautiful new cowboy boots with Ken Hagin Jr. feverishly wiping the sticky clay from them as the "Praise the Lord" theme echoed down the halls of Channel 14! The problem had been caused by our parking lot repaving project. Only half of the asphalt had been laid—the other half was "Oklahoma red" and it had just rained. Dad's car had been parked on the edge of the new parking lot and as he got out—well, you can guess the rest!

Needless to say, we did not take any leg shots of Dad that night—nor even any long shots for that matter. But all in all, Dad was a good sport and we all pitched in to get him cleaned up enough for the program. Dad was vintage Hagin that night as he taught us the word of "FAITH" as only he can. The viewers never knew that Dad's feet were planted firmly in material that looked more like red brick by the end of the three hour program.

As fate would have it, Dad, Ken Jr., Merv, and I all bumped into each other at the corner of two halls as Dad was leaving for home. Ken Jr. called out to Merv in his inimitable Oklahoma drawl, *"Go git the ker, Merv—and this time don't park her in the mud so that diddy gits his feet muddy!"* Merv exited hastily amid peals of laughter from several TBN staffers who were within earshot.

This phrase—*"Go git the ker"* has since been immortalized by the staff of TBN and has been broadened, mainly by the engineers, as requests are issued to, *"go git"* most anything from a pencil to a "Holy Beamer."

Sadly, Merv's tenure at the Hagin Ministries did not last long and we learned that he had moved from job to job finally deciding to start a secular singing career. When that did not prove successful he finally called and persuaded me to meet him for lunch. At that meeting, Merv requested that I consider rehiring him for a position back at TBN. I explained that while none of us at TBN held any ill will toward him and had unconditionally forgiven him for his previous attacks, there would probably never be another job for him at TBN. When I made this abundantly clear, Merv's attitude changed dramatically and he advised me that he would now take his story to the secular media—*"60 Minutes," "20/20,"* or one of several exposé type TV shows. He also threatened to write a book which, in his NRB letter, he said would be titled, "Godfathers of the Gospel." I told Merv as we parted for the last time on this earth, that I still loved him and forgave him for all of his anger and seeming hatred of TBN and me.

Merv's "exposé" was never made nor was his book

written. A few months after his final attack through the NRB, Merv died of cancer at 46 years of age. All we could do was the same we had done for Ward Vanguard—commit him into the hands of a loving and merciful Lord and move on.

The final round of allegations to the NRB turned into a veritable insane asylum! New charges came from Ray Wilson, better known as "Black Buffalo," producer of a children's TV program. Fifteen year old charges were dredged up from my days of employment at Faith Center including a number of false allegations that ranged from stealing the church mailing list to cheating widows and orphans out of their life savings!   All of this had been disproved and laid to rest years ago, but here came the charges again, *and all carefully timed and leaked to the news media to gain maximum exposure!*

I called Jerry Rose who was then president of NRB. I pled with him to order the face-to-face meeting which I had demanded by letter to Richard Bott so that we could settle this uproar as brothers in Christ, but to no avail. The sad truth—TBN was put on TRIAL by my Christian brothers through carefully timed and expertly orchestrated leaks, interviews and releases to *the secular media!* I still grieve for a lost and dying world whose only glimpse of Jesus was a Christian lynching party out to get one of their own brothers! My numerous pleas for a face-to-face meeting with my accusers was first ignored and finally turned down. My pleas to follow the scriptural mandate were denied:

To NRB, Or Not To NRB

Brethren, if a man be overtaken
in a fault, ye which are spiritual,
restore such an one in the spirit of
meekness; considering thyself,
lest thou also be tempted.
Galatians 6:1

In the depths of this maelstrom of charges, counter-charges, lies, and scandalous media reports, a word of wisdom came to me from your mother. It was written in her own hand. It was folded neatly and lying on my Bible where she knew I would find it the next morning at my prayer time.

> Paul, God chose you to carry the cross of being hurt in the press so that others who go through this can be ministered to by *you!*

> God looked all over His world and found someone that would go through this trial and would not get discouraged or give up! God loved you so much, He trusted *you* with this and knew you would not "blow it" for Him.

> If I can, you can!

> I love you—Jan.

Tawny and Laurie, you too, may be called upon to turn the tide from defeat to victory for Paul Jr. and Matthew. I can tell you that Jan's word of encouragement just may have made the difference for me at a very critical moment in my life. I will be forever grateful for her obedience to the Holy Spirit. It is also at times like these that your love for each other grows stronger and deeper than ever.

Finally, after nearly two years of charges, counter-charges, rumors, and exhaustive investigation and examination of mountains of documents, the NRB Executive Committee issued this terse statement in December of 1991:

> After reviewing the materials made available to it, the Committee finds there is insufficient evidence to warrant termination of membership.

I immediately tendered my resignation to the NRB which prompted another whole round of media stories and speculations.

Well, my sons, there you have it—perhaps the saddest chapter of these first 20 years for TBN. Mostly because of the sick and twisted perception that the world received from CHRISTIANS! I am sure, as a result, many turned a deaf ear to our message—I pray none will be lost from Christ because of my actions even though they were uttered in defense of the truth as I saw and understood it.

To NRB, Or Not To NRB

And yet, there is a brighter ending to this chapter than you might expect. First of all, there are MANY good and godly members of the NRB. Most are still my dear friends and brothers in Christ. The rest I have forgiven and hold no bitterness toward—may God be my witness. Remember, my sons, unforgiveness and bitterness only hurt the one who holds on to it. The one you are bitter against may not even be aware of *your* problem. Besides, forgiveness is NOT an option if you choose to be a true follower of Jesus Christ. He, Himself, said:

> *For if ye forgive men their trespasses,*
> *your heavenly Father will also forgive*
> *you: But if ye forgive not men their*
> *trespasses, neither will your Father*
> *forgive your trespasses.*
> *Matthew 6:14, 15*

I know, in the natural, that it is difficult most of the time to forgive those who have hurt you, but just remember this: forgiveness is simply a choice—I choose to forgive and when I do something wonderful happens—suddenly, I AM FREE! There is even a medical dimension to unforgiveness and bitterness as Dr. Donald Whitaker and Dr. Reginald Cherry and others have taught us. It literally creates a physical and chemical imbalance which contributes to a whole host of other physical ailments from ulcers to cancer! So learn this lesson well, my sons—*FORGIVE*—there are

NO options. Finally, when you make the decision to forgive—God ALWAYS gives you the ability to release the hurt, the pain, or the grief to Him!

Another positive aspect to this whole ordeal might be drawn from the fact that nearly two years of digging and investigation of TBN turned up *"INSUFFICIENT EVIDENCE TO WARRANT TERMINATION OF MEMBERSHIP."* Pretty high praise, I'd say—how about you? Another very interesting by-line to this point came from another former enemy. Do you remember Mr. John Virtue of our Saddleback chapter? During the NRB's time of probing for scandal about TBN and me, a prominent newspaper reporter called Mr. Virtue knowing that he and his group had probed for nearly five years into the very heart of TBN. Mr. Virtue sent me a copy of a letter that he wrote to the editor of *The Los Angeles Times*. In his letter he recounted the conversation in which he informed a very disappointed newspaper reporter that he should give up on his search for dirt concerning TBN and me. Mr. Virtue's letter speaks for itself and included the following:

> I read with disappointment your recent article concerning Paul Crouch, and his activities in Christian broadcasting.
>
> My impression is that your reporter entered into an investigation hoping to find material of a damaging nature, on

the order of the recent scandals involving other Christian broadcasters.

I was interviewed by your reporter in connection with the article, and my impression of your negative approach arose because of the nature of the questions, which were essentially a search for material damaging to Mr. Crouch.

The reason for my interview was, that for several years, I headed a group that filed a challenge with the Federal Communications Commission to the license of the Santa Ana television station owned by the Paul Crouch broadcasting group. During that time, in connection with our challenge, we made an investigation, and searched for background information, that would be damaging to Mr. Crouch or his organization. We found no negative information, only positive information.

I informed your reporter of this, and further informed him that during our license challenge, Mr. Crouch was at all times a gentleman, polite, and sincere in his beliefs. The reporter told me that he

had heard this from other parties he had
interviewed.

My disappointment with your article is
that as I read it, I looked for some
positive results from the investigation,
but only found the negatives.

The article, although not materially
damaging either to Mr. Crouch or his
activities, raised doubts because *The
Times* printed it in a non objective
manner, and many readers, hoping to
find negative news about Christian
broadcasting, found solace in the fact
that it was printed in this fashion.

I thanked Mr. Virtue most heartily for this good
report and also for letting me know of it.

And finally, your mother and I even accepted
formal Christian conciliation with Heath Kaiser who
had participated in the whole NRB ordeal. The result
was total and unconditional forgiveness and release of
all bitterness and claims toward each other for the past.
But, of course, that never made the papers or any of the
secular media.

By the way, I still hold out the hand of fellowship to
the NRB just as Joseph did to his brothers!

So, is there life after NRB? Read on, my sons, and
I'll paint for you a picture of such glory for the future,

TO NRB, OR NOT TO NRB

it may take your breath away!
  Dad's last chapter is next!

CHAPTER 24

EPILOGUE

So, my sons, where do we go from here? *Ah, this is where it gets really exciting!* So what were these first twenty years of spiritual conflict for? Was God testing us and trying us just to build a great Christian TV network for us American, English speaking souls? *Well—partly!* Was God just wanting to show HIS mighty power to save and deliver His TV network from its many enemies? *Well, yes, but read on!* Would God have allowed us to pass through these deep waters, fiery trials, and lions' dens just to reach about ten percent of the population of the earth living here in North America? *I think not!*

Actually, the grand design—even the grand finale for TBN began, of all places, at the 1983 Full Gospel Businessmen's World Convention in Detroit, Michigan. Your mother and I were there with the "Holy Beamer," sending the great messages and spiritual events of the convention to the TBN satellite network. As we waited for the broadcast to begin, a Christian businessman from the island of St. Maarten in the eastern Caribbean islands approached us. Sir Charles Vlaun had been knighted by Queen Beatrix of the Netherlands and had served for a time as prime minister of the island. He was now a successful businessman, but characteristic of the Full Gospel Businessmen, had been conducting luncheons and banquets throughout the Caribbean islands. In the course of his ministry, Sir Charles had made friends with the prime minister of the Island of Nevis, a British crown colony to the south of St. Maarten. Simeon Daniel and Sir Charles had met at a Full Gospel Businessmen's luncheon and had discussed the possibility of a Christian radio station to reach the islands and especially Cuba which was, then, solidly a Russian communist client state. Mr. Daniel, a Christian brother, had indicated the willingness of his government to grant broadcasting licenses to Christians who might be willing to invest in such a venture. As a final, prophetic afterthought, Sir Charles asked, "What if we could attract investors who would be willing to build a Christian TV station?" The prime minister assured him the invitation would include licenses to operate a TV station as well.

My sons, you are here witnessing the embryonic stages of God's great MASTER PLAN for a Christian TV network much, much bigger than any of us had ever imagined up to that point. Your Grandpa Bethany had caught a little gleam of it as he knelt in the waist-high weeds of our vacant lot in Tustin, California back in 1975. As he lifted his hands in praise, I heard him declare, "This will be the WORLD HEADQUARTERS for the Trinity Broadcasting Network!" I remember how strange his words sounded to me then as we struggled to get our FIRST TV station underway for southern California!

I am not sure that Sir Charles Vlaun even knew of TBN as he discussed the possibility of a Christian radio, and now a TV station, with Prime Minister Simeon Daniel of Nevis Island, but I am sure that God arranged our meeting with Sir Charles at the 1983 Full Gospel Businessmen's Convention in Detroit! During offerings and announcements we broke away to the TBN set behind the platform for TV ministry and testimonies. Someone introduced us to Sir Charles Vlaun who brought interesting news and greetings from the Full Gospel Businessmen of the eastern Caribbean islands. As we chatted he told of the opportunity for Christian TV in a foreign land I had never even heard of—Nevis, St. Christopher Islands, halfway between Miami and Venezuela, South America! *Wonder of wonders*, on LIVE TV from Detroit, Michigan, the Holy Spirit began to unfold God's great plan—Christian TV, not just for America, but even for foreign lands! I remember sending word during the live interview to Ben Miller, our director of engineering, asking if he could give us an estimate of the cost to build a VHF TV station on Nevis Island. In a few minutes a note was handed to me—approximately $400,000 for basic transmission equipment.

Looking back, now, I can see how unbusinesslike it was to throw out a call to our partners without further study and investigation of this "opportunity," but the spark ignited—the Holy Spirit gave witness and the phones back home in California began to ring! By the end of the program, Jay Jones, our prayer partner director, had called us in Detroit with the overwhelming news: *"You passed the $400,000 mark an hour ago and the phones are still ringing!"* Without a doubt, God had confirmed *our FIRST* step on to foreign soil with a TBN TV station—*it would be Nevis-St. Christopher* from which we would cover a vast region of the eastern Caribbean islands with the Gospel—LIVE via satellite! We shook hands with Sir Charles Vlaun on the spot and made plans to journey as soon as possible to meet Prime Minister Simeon Daniel and the other government officials of Nevis Island. A few weeks later when we arrived in Nevis, to our great delight, we were received warmly and within hours our application and plans were underway for this LAST great phase of Trinity Broadcasting Network.

One heart-wrenching story must be told here which made this new venture all the more poignant. It actually involved the largest single gift that TBN had received to that point. When I received Mr. and Mrs. Wilbur Lantz into my office in July of 1983, I could not have imagined the tragic circumstances that surrounded their most generous gift of $400,000! Their precious daughters, Karen and Julie, age six and eight, had lost their lives in a flaming auto accident. Mother and dad were miraculously spared, but the light of their lives had been snuffed out! The check handed to me that day was part of a large settlement they had received from a nationally known firm. Their only request was that this first foreign TBN station be dedicated to the memory of their precious daughters, Karen Elain and Julie Ann Lantz. That dedicatory plaque has welcomed each visitor to TBN Channel 13, Nevis, West Indies each and every day since its birth. The Lantz family wanted their gift to make Satan pay dearly for taking their children, and they could not think of a better way than a 24-hour Christian TV station, and TBN's first foreign missions station at that! By the way, did you notice the amount? $400,000 was exactly the amount needed to get the transmission equipment *ON THE AIR!* The other gifts enabled us to build the needed TV studio for production of local programs as well. I firmly believe that God gives us these extra signposts along the way to let us know that we are right on course!

It seemed that this first foreign station breakthrough was the key to what I have been calling the LAST great phase for TBN. We had tried prior to Nevis to get foreign stations going, but with little success. We did buy time on a station in Haiti for French "Praise the Lord," and Nora Lam had produced Chinese "Praise the Lord" for many years which is still seen each week in Taiwan. But the idea of a WHOLE TBN Christian TV station operating on foreign soil was a dream that seemed out of reach. Many foreign governments were willing to talk to us, but to give a broadcasting license to an American Christian TV network–*well, who was this TBN?* And, much more importantly, *what would they do with it?* Most world governments still maintain very tight control over their TV channels, knowing the powerful influence TV has on its viewers!

But now—to our delight, doors to foreign nations began to open up! Yes, I will always know that Nevis was the key—a mighty spiritual offensive had been launched—a glorious breakthrough into Satan's cherished domain—the AIRWAVES OF THE WORLD!

Next came El Salvador—how we fought—five long years, but we won! Channel 25 flashed on the air in 1990. In the midst of many other battles we loaded up our little aircraft, "Eagle I," and flew most of a whole TV station to a Christian group in Guatemala City and Channel 21 flashed on the air!

Remember, that the tempo was increasing dramatically here at home, too, and since the late 1980's TBN has averaged about ONE NEW TV STATION A WEEK—ON THE AIR! God knew we would need an ever expanding base here at home to support the new foreign stations coming on line.

Next was Italy! Missionary Frank Farnsworth put us in touch with the owner of a TV station in Campione, Italy, a city on the border of Switzerland. It covered Lugano, Switzerland plus it had two other low power stations that covered much of the northern Italian border region. Later we were able to purchase a major station in the heart of northern Italy—*Milan!* By last count, twelve stations cover most of northern Italy—*now it's on to Rome!* One exciting footnote to Italy was a miracle we did not even realize was happening at the time. As we were finalizing the purchase of our first station in Campione, we formed a new corporation which we named TBNE—*Trinity Broadcasting Network of Europe!* Scarcely had we formed the corporation and secured the station, when Italian law changed, and today we could not even have such a corporation! But an even greater miracle has come to pass that ONLY God could have known of and arranged. In 1993, the first phase of the EC or *European Community* has come into being. Since Italy is a member of the new EC, TBNE is now qualified legally to do business in all of western Europe! *Germany—here we come*, as well as all of the twelve member nations. Oh, what a God we serve—one who knows the end from the beginning—the Lord of the harvest is in control—*Praise the Lord!*

In the middle of all of this growth and victory, Ambassador Douw Steyn came from South Africa with an invitation to build *AFRICA'S FIRST* Christian TV station! The state of Ciskei in South Africa had received its independence from the Republic of South Africa. Its president, Mr. Lennox Sebe, was willing to grant a license for an all Christian TV station. Again, it was the missionaries Reverend and Mrs. Philip Ray who had been Ambassador Steyn's pastors, that brought us all together. Much more could be written of the awesome battles and sacrifices made by both

Americans and Africans to see this miracle brought to birth. The historic news broke in December of 1986—*Channel 24 Ciskei, South Africa—ON THE AIR!* Soon, the Transkei next door was calling, followed by an invitation by the SABC—the South African Broadcasting Company—to place 26 hours a month of Christian programming on the national network, covering the *whole of southern Africa!* Surely all Heaven rejoiced to see Africa opening up to Christian television! The word spread quickly and Namibia, South West Africa requested programming, followed by Swaziland, Zaire, and Zambia. Even as I write, Uganda, and Nigeria are calling! Evangelist Reinhard Bonnke is right, "ALL OF AFRICA SHALL BE SAVED!"

But, my sons, none of us were prepared for the collapse of the Iron Curtain and the opening of Russia to, not only the Gospel, but—*CHRISTIAN TELEVISION!* Another book would be required to tell of our meetings with the Mayor of Leningrad, now St. Petersburg—plus the many trips and negotiating sessions—but the glorious news I share with you today—*St. Petersburg, Channel 40 is ON THE AIR and Moscow is coming soon!* We have conducted five giant crusades in Moscow, St. Petersburg, and Kiev and seen literally thousands come to Christ as John Jacobs, The Power Team, Jeff Fenholt, Dino Kartsonakis, Laverne and Edith Tripp, Walt and Betty Mills, plus many others, have invaded Russia with the Gospel.

Time nor space will let me tell you the full stories of *Athens, Corinth, and Thessalonica, Greece; Costa Rica,*

Nicaragua, Honduras, Belize; La Paz, Bolivia, and Buenos Aires, Argentina! Praise God, all are ON THE AIR and growing with new stations spreading to other cities and countries of Central and South America.

Finally the last bastion that seemed the most impossible of all—*CHINA!* As we celebrate the first twenty years of God's great victories, we are in the final stages of our first TV station in the southernmost province of *THE PEOPLE'S REPUBLIC OF CHINA* in Hainan Island!

Add to all of this our major motion picture, CHINA CRY, that is now being distributed worldwide in foreign languages, plus SUPER POWER KTBN short wave radio station—just in case we missed somebody, and there you have it, my dear sons—*a voice like no other in the HISTORY OF THE WORLD—MIGHTY TBN, your voice, my voice, God's voice, going into ALL the world, preaching the GOSPEL to every creature!*

But there remains ONE LAST unanswered question in this master plan to reach our world with the message of Jesus Christ—*how do we speak to them in the languages that they can understand?*

ENTER God's final solution to the international language barrier: *TBN's IPC—yes, the International Production Center,* which we dedicate in the year of our Lord—1993. Translation rooms with the latest state-of-the-art technology, translators to make R.W. Schambach, E.V. Hill, Benny Hinn, Dwight Thompson, Reinhard Bonnke, plus a host of TBN programmers— SPEAK IN THE LANGUAGES OF THE NATIONS!

A facility so unique there is no other like it in the world!

Ah, my sons, do you finally see God's great strategy? God's final solution—the answer to the Apostle Paul's burning question: *"How shall they hear without a preacher?"* Yes, God's master plan is becoming gloriously apparent. TV stations at home and abroad, satellites, "holy beamers," short wave radio, long wave radio, satellite dishes, cable stations, and now, *THEY CAN ALL SPEAK IN OTHER TONGUES!*

Years ago, your Grandpa Bethany used to say, "Children, put on your faith glasses." We could hardly understand this when we were trying to see even *one* TV station by faith! But, now, even Papa's "faith glasses" are not needed—*WE SEE IT!* God's great *MASTER PLAN* is clear! Today we stand on God's launching pad like the mighty space missiles on Cape Canaveral!

Praise God, the smoke, steam, and fire of the Holy Spirit is pouring from every fibre and pore of our beings! *FIVE...FOUR...THREE...TWO...IGNITION!!!* Yes, we are ON OUR WAY! We will not rest until every soul on planet earth receives the message of salvation in his own language through GOD'S MIRACLE OF TBN! *Praise the Lord!*

My sons, I truly believe that this could be that FINAL generation that all of the prophets of old spoke of. I believe that before another twenty years have passed, we will all be rejoicing around the Great Throne of God! But, if not, in a very few short years I will pass the torch to YOU and I am confident that you, and even my children's children, will carry this GOOD NEWS to the very ends of the EARTH. *In that day you, too, will have no father but God.*

I love you—Godspeed. *Maranatha!*

Sincerely,

Dad

And further, by these, my son, be admonished: of making many books there is no end; and much study is a weariness of the flesh. Let us hear the conclusion of the whole matter: Fear God, and keep his commandments: for this is the whole duty of man. For God shall bring every work into judgment, with every secret thing, whether it be good, or whether it be evil.
Ecclesiastes 12:12-14

My two sons, **Paul Jr.** and **Matthew** on Matt's wedding day, August 25, 1985. You have to be a father of two fine young sons like these to know the joy they bring. Now you know where they got their good looks!

My father's mother, your great grandmother, **Agnes Leaming Crouch**. There has been no greater saint of God. Those eyes…those eyes.

My mother and father—**Sarah Matilda** and **Andrew Franklin Crouch**.

My father, **Andrew Crouch** in Egypt, being carried as we boarded the ship for home in 1939. His heart had become so weakened, the doctor ordered him not to climb stairs.

My German nurse, **Heidi Hanover,** with me at age seven, shortly before my father died.

KCBI — our pioneer radio station at **Central Bible Institute** in Springfield, Missouri. With 50 whole watts we signed her on with, *"Hello World!"*

Our *"BIG DAY,"* August 25, 1957. **Papa Bethany** honored us with a classic wedding at his church, North Highland Assembly in Columbus, Georgia. He and Jan's mother, **Laurie Elizabeth** are at the left. To the right is my mother, **Sarah Matilda** and my brother-in-law **Bernard Ridings**.

August 25, 1957, our "BIG DAY."

How I wish I could have kept you both this age — forever! **Matt**, we finally broke you from sucking your thumb — by bribery! **Paul Jr.**, you were your baby brother's best protector ever!

Jan, **Paul Jr.**, **Mom Bethany**, **Matt** and **Papa**—about 1968.

The Assemblies of God received an award for its first TV series, *Men With a Mission*, hosted by Willard Cantelon. The Winona Lake Film Festival honored (from left) producer **Jan Sadlo**; Foreign Missions Director **Noel Perkin**; myself as assistant producer; and Promotions Director **Phillip Hogan**.

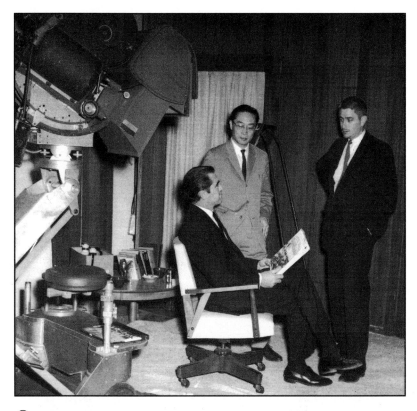

On the set of the Assemblies of God TV and Film Production Studio in Burbank, California. In addition to the church's productions we did occasional work for the U.S. Army's TV series *The Big Picture*. Actor **Steve Cochran** is pictured seated here.

Mayor **H.I. Froseth** of Corona, California while I was
general manager of KREL radio. We thought the World's
Fair was coming to Corona in 1967. It didn't!

Matthew and **Paul Jr.**, do you remember borrowing my *Behind the Scenes* director's chair to help shoot a documentary film for your school class project? Would you please return my chair?

Cameras and making pictures were "in the blood!" **Matthew**, you borrowed my 8mm film camera and a tripod from Channel 40 for your school class project. The grade?...<u>A</u> of course!

My two sons, **Matthew** (left) and **Paul Jr.** (between Mickey and Minnie Mouse). Disneyland was a rare treat!

With all of the criticism of TV evangelists, I like to remind everyone that Jan and I still live in our same home we purchased for $38,500 in 1971, two years before TBN was born. I guess now we have to be careful we do not get proud of our humility! This photo was taken in 1973. Please, **Jan** — more pictures on the wall!

Mighty **Mt. Wilson** just above Los Angeles, California. I will always know that God moved part of that mountain for our first TV broadcast — May 28, 1973.

Our first rented **studio** at 111 W. Dyer Road in Santa Ana, California. I prayed on this roof and a "mountain" moved! Our first *Praise the Lord* program aired from here — May 28, 1973.

Jan and **Tammy Bakker** scraping up tile and tar for our first TV studio at 111 W. Dyer Road in Santa Ana, California. **Tammy Sue** lends moral support at left.

1973, our first **Family Christmas TV Special**. Our set was composed of the Christmas cards from our wonderful pioneer partners.

In 1973 **Jim Bakker**, **Rod Henke** and I took turns hosting and co-hosting the *Praise* program. Some nights when no one else was available we were also the *guests!* **Jan** was our main telephone prayer partner.

Behind the Scenes — our second longest running TBN program! The table on the right was part of our home bedroom set.

Paul **Jr.** you needed a haircut! But in those early days there was no time as everyone pitched in to get TBN on the air!

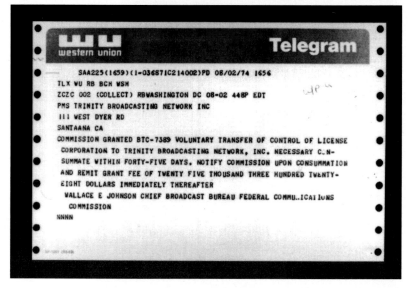

O̲ur first **FCC telegram** granting the license of Channel 40 to TBN in southern California—August 2, 1974—Praise the Lord!

August 2, 1974, the **FCC telegram** finally came! I picked it up personally and we claimed our first TV station, Channel 40, in southern California.

Jan and I with board members, **Demos Shakarian**, **Paul Toberty** and **Norman Juggert**. Live *Praise the Lord* in our new studio in Tustin, California. We moved in on Easter Sunday of 1976.

One of our early TBN rallies at the Anaheim Convention Center, Anaheim, California. 10,000-plus turned out for *their* TV station as we had "OLD TIME REVIVAL!"

(714) 731-1000

Believe it or not this is actually **Jerry Bernard** lying exhausted on the TBN Praise-A-Thon set. He had just sung *It's Real* for the 8th time straight by popular demand. Those were the days!

This picture should have been burned! Jan said we should remember the telethon where **Dwight Thompson** preached, **Zonelle** played the organ, **Jan** played the vibraharp and I played piano! No one was calling so one dear partner called to say, *"We will all pledge if you will all stop playing!"* So, we did.

Michelle at
Chambers,
Tustin,
California, site
of our new TV
studio.

Papa Bethany (Jan's Dad) and I as work began on our new
TV studio in Tustin, California.

Paul **Toberty** and I along with hundreds of wonderful partners broke ground for our new studio in late 1975.

Paul **Jr.** recording the progress on our second **TBN studio** which we built in Tustin, California. Twenty years later he is *still* recording!

What a day! The fall of 1977, local pastors joined **Jan** and me as we dedicated **Channel 21** to the Lord in Phoenix, Arizona.

What a night! Each white slip is a soul receiving Jesus as personal Saviour. Thank you, **Hal Lindsey** and *ALL* who have helped us through the years bringing *MULTITUDES* to Christ.

April 10, 1978, our mighty new **satellite station** signed *ON THE AIR!* We anointed it with Holy Land oil as hundreds helped dedicate it to the Lord! *"And I saw another angel..."* *Revelation 14:6.*

This picture, taken while our main satellite station was being built surprised us all. It was not retouched or double exposed. This *light from the heavens* is still a mystery!

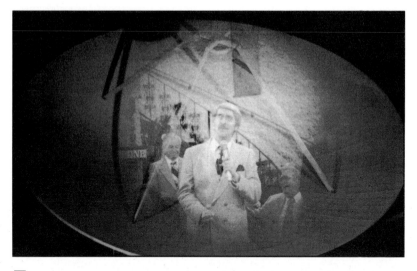

This unusual double exposure seemed strangely prophetic. The mighty satellite dish is still beaming *Praise* to much of the world.

Many thousands assembled in **Washington, D.C.** on April 29, 1980 for a day of prayer for our nation.

The Oval office — it's clear the **President** is more interested in the camera than in me!

The day we met **Queen Elizabeth II** and **Prince Philip** in Nevis. I spoke to her briefly about TBN and pointed out our TV station just across the road from the Governor General's house. It seems I am still looking at the station!

We were honored to meet **Pope John Paul II** in Rome and speak to him briefly *(real briefly)* about TBN. With me was **Norm Juggert**, our TBN secretary and attorney, and you **Matthew**.

John **Jacobs** and the **Power Team** with me in Russia. I'm the one in the middle!

Joy flows from the "Four Corners" of America on special nights like this. **Rich** and **Robin Wilkerson, Carlton Pearson, Jan** and I, and **Laverne** and **Edith Tripp** lead the TBN family in special prayer as we reach out to our "Whole Wide World."

Matt, the night you actually proposed to **Laurie** on LIVE TV! I think you knew pretty much what the answer would be.

After 36 years we are still **sweethearts**! We were not to be out done even on Matt and Laurie's wedding day— August 25, 1985.

Our precious grandchildren have brought a whole new dimension of joy to our lives. *Right:* Our first grandson, Brandon Paul, enjoying a "piggyback" ride with his PaPa. *Below:* With Brandon Paul Crouch, III and Miss Brittany Brianne Crouch.

There are no words to describe the delight that a grandbaby brings. Little Carra Linda Crouch is the newest blessing in our family!

My pride and joy, **"Prince"** — pure white Arabian stallion. I'm ready for the "Second Coming"!

The Crouch clan in December of 1992 from left-to-right: *back row* — **Paul Jr.**, **Tawny**, **Jan** and **Matthew**; *front row* — **Brandon**, **Brittany**, **Carra Linda**, Dad, **Caylan** and **Laurie**.